Beyond the Wedding Vows

CARMELLA ANTONINO

Pittsburgh, PA

ISBN 1-58501-061-8

Trade Paperback
©Copyright 2001 Carmella Antonino
All rights reserved
First Printing—2001
Library of Congress #99-69662

Request for information should be addressed to:

CeShore Publishing Company
The Sterling Building
440 Friday Road
Pittsburgh, PA 15209
www.ceshore.com

CeShore is an imprint of SterlingHouse Publisher, Inc.
Cover design: Michelle S. Lenkner—SterlingHouse Publisher
Page Design: Bernadette Kazmarski

Printed in Canada

Table of Contents

Dedication

This book is dedicated to my husband Gary,

of twenty-four years, thank you for your

vision, patience and love; to Lauren, my

daughter, an original independent woman

with great tenacity and spirit; and Mark, my

son, a sensitive and responsible man with a

brilliant future.

I LOVE YOU ALL MOST DEARLY.

In Loving Memory of
John Catalano

Acknowledgements

I especially want to thank Cynthia Sterling. Without Cynthia's vision, support, guidance and enthusiasm for this project, this book would not exist. I am grateful to her.

Thank you to Megan Davidson, my editor, for her many challenges and detailed critiques. Megan gave her extraordinary talent and expertise without hesitation to make this book as responsive as possible to the needs of our readers.

Thank you to Jennifer Piemme, Chelley Lenkner (Cover Design) and Annick Rouzier of Sterling House for their time, talents and assistance.

Thank you to the many women who shared their stories unselfishly and openly.

A very special thanks to my mother, Sylvia, who taught me through example, to respect the courage of my convictions and perseverance.

Thank you to my sisters Connie George and Tina Yerman Wingate and to my special sisters Marie McKibben, Peg Knapp, Devra Bastiaens and Pat Werner.

I am grateful to all for their encouragement support and love. Sisters are priceless gifts from God and I am blessed to have them.

Thank you to Emily and Miles Pavlovic, Becky Yerman, and Nicole and Stephanie Antonino for their encouragement and support. They hold a special place in my heart.

Special gratitude goes to my confidant for encouragement and support especially in assisting me to clarify my insights regarding cultural stereotyping.

Most importantly to Gary, my husband, and Lauren and Mark, my children, for their patience, support and love. And thank you for leaving me alone to struggle through the writing.

Important Notice:

The author has changed the names and all identifying characteristics of every woman and man whose story is told in this book.

Introduction

"Adultery is a meanness and a stealing, a taking away from
someone what should be theirs, a great selfishness, and surrounded
and guarded by lies it should be found out. And out of the
meanness and selfishness and lying, flow love and joy and peace
beyond anything that can be imagined."
Dame Rose Macaulay (1881–1958)

This book is nonjudgmental. The information contained in
this book is not intended to endorse or deny anyone's choice
in matters of the heart. It is up to each individual to define
her moral and ethical standards and put them into play.
The path of each individual's life is unique and unpredictable. One may discover that nothing in life is steadfast,
guaranteed or impenetrable, especially belief systems. No
one is excluded from the many lessons of life, and even a
saint will have her beliefs challenged.

It cannot be denied that extra-marital affairs exist. There
is a coarsening of American culture that is having an effect
on sexual behavior. This book addresses the changing standards of how we view extra-marital affairs. Regardless of
the attitude or position you take on extra-marital affairs or
whether you are considering to have or have had an extra-
marital affair you will find this book invaluable because it

presents comprehensive interpretations that reflect a re-search synopsis of essential information needed to make an informed choice.

This book will remain objective and not critical—a guide to provide insight and understanding into the consequences one can garner, good or bad, if the decision to have an af-fair or end an affair is on your agenda. Many women who have engaged in extra-marital affairs have become victims. The purpose of this book is to provide information for women to evaluate and examine, in order to prevent them from becoming victims of their own choices.

Many of the issues presented in this book can also per-tain to our homosexual friends who may find this informa-tion helpful. The information crosses gender and sexual orientation.

Questioning the existence of God and an individual's pur-pose, as well as wondering whether or not there's a point to the world is both normal and healthy. Who's to say why some people struggle harder than others to find answers to questions that plague them? It often seems the more noble and idealistic a person, the harder it is for her to accept the consequences of her actions.

To a woman who is involved in an extra-marital relation-ship, the world becomes a confusing place. What used to make sense is now senseless and what held value is now without worth. It is horrifying when a woman learns that she is capable of lying, neglecting the needs of her children, spouse, family and friends, in order to steal a few hours with another man. The shock a woman experiences when she discovers it is possible to love two men at one time is a be-trayal of the highest order. This realization is like a dreaded disease; it's supposed to happen to someone else.

A woman who finds herself involved on any level of an extra-marital relationship questions everything from her own sanity to the concepts of love and marriage. At some point she realizes that her innocence is lost, her white knight is only a man, her youthful ideas of love and romance must give way to a mature outlook. The difficult part of the whole process is acceptance. Choices and change are two things we cannot escape, so we must learn to embrace, enjoy and be enthusiastic about them.

Choices have consequences. Decision-making demands a tremendous amount of responsibility and accountability. Our choices shape our character and our character determines our choices; therefore, these two elements are so deeply intertwined and highly dependent upon each other that they simply cannot be separated. The intent of this book is to help you, the reader, live in harmony with who you are and the decisions you make.

Spiritual, emotional, mental and physical crises happen to all of us, and when they do, our entire world can fall apart. Very few of us escape life without these valuable experiences. While we are feeling the pressure, confusion, disruption and pain of change and crisis, it is almost impossible to understand the benefit. We are often faced with more than one life-altering event in our lives, but nothing compares to the magic and danger of adultery. It has been said that what does not kill us makes us stronger, and surviving an extra-marital affair will make a woman stronger— if she chooses to learn from experience.

Sadly, many women choose to remain blind, deaf and dumb when it comes to matters of the heart. Perhaps this is because when dealing with love we think it is permissible to act without consulting our intellectual, spiritual and physical needs. When people ignore any one part of their being, trouble is likely to occur.

Unfortunately, we do not live in a world of "black and white," and the line between good and bad is often zig-zagged and blurry. For example, let's examine the premise that it is wrong for one human to kill another. Very few people disagree that killing is not only wrong but also immoral. However, according to our laws, there are times when killing another human being is acceptable. Even our religious leaders who preach "thou shalt not kill", agree with the non-secular lawmakers. The "wrongness" of killing is measured in degrees ranging from: noble (killing the enemy to defend your country); to justifiable (defending your life); to forgivable (crime of passion); to understandable (protecting your possessions or property); to compassionate (euthanasia); to extenuating (mentally or emotionally maladjusted); to an accident (manslaughter); to calculated (first, second or third degree murder). Most people, however, do not accept killing as a justification for a crime of passion, protecting property and possessions, euthanasia, mental or emotional maladjustment, accidental, or calculated murder because they believe that they are all contestable motives for killing.

If killing is acceptable under certain circumstances, then it is not surprising that, in certain situations, adultery is also excepted from the moral code. Adultery becomes acceptable, forgivable and almost encouraged if the spouse is abusive, unfaithful or unable to perform conjugal obligations.

It would be so easy if life had absolutes. It is absolutely wrong to kill! It is absolutely wrong to steal! It is absolutely wrong to commit adultery! But, there are no absolutes, only exceptions to both God's and man's laws. This leaves most of us floundering in a world of our own making. This is where choices and consequences come into play.

The key word that we will be dealing with throughout this book is choices. We all have them and we alone must make them. No one can force his or her will upon us without our consent.

The catch here is simple: You are responsible for choices, so you must somehow find the courage to accept and deal with the consequences. Actually, when you look at it, making a choice is the easy part. The hard part is living with the results. Even when you make a good choice, you will have some adjusting and readjusting to do. Often when a person makes a decision, it is not immediately apparent if it was a good one, or how it will affect a person's life.

Some people argue that, once you make the right decision, you will have a gut feeling you were right and will feel a sense of peace. That is a wonderful thought, but often we don't listen to what our "gut" is telling us. The feeling of peace may merely be a result of finally coming to some sort of decision. Normally it is only in retrospect that we can honestly evaluate our choices. Once we stand back and are removed from the thick of the forest we can finally see the trees and the forest they comprise. In essence, not seeing the forest through the trees is being lost. When we are lost, we panic and make mistakes. A woman living and loving outside her marriage should prepare herself for the dark nights ahead and the journey through the forest. This book is a survival manual for the journey beyond the wedding wows.

Women not only take advantage of their five senses, they have a vast capacity to utilize their sixth sense of intuition, which, according to Webster's dictionary, is "direct perception of truth, fact, etc. independent of any reasoning process." Since women have so much going for them, they must wake from the stupor that dulls their senses and develop the "artist within" who is creative, directed and confident enough to paint her own canvas. They need to be aware of their feelings, use their intellect, develop their intuition and start consciously shaping the world to meet their goals, dreams and visions. If an affair is going to help you do this, then who's to judge whether it is right or wrong? But, if a woman is entering into an affair hoping that somebody else can make all this happen for her, she is in big trouble.

Before entering into a liaison, a woman must weigh her choices and potential consequences. If she is doing anything less, she is not acting in her own best interest. A woman cannot afford to make choices wearing blinders. It is not acceptable to blame others. She must start conducting life as an adult by doing her due diligence, that is a careful and thorough effort, to be aware of all of the potential consequences that an extra-marital affair will bring. If this sounds like a calculated approach to having an affair, it is.

We, as women, do feel a deep sense of responsibility, commitment, devotion and an overall reverence for life. Becoming aware of our choices and consequences, and taking full responsibility for them, will indeed affirm our existence, build our character and help us express our creativity. If we are doing those things—whether or not we are having an extra-marital affair—we will find courage and develop a noble heart.

This book is the result of a research compendium that addresses possible issues before the fact of an affair, through the process of circumstances, choices and consequences of an affair, to after the fact of an affair. The author did not create these extremes; they already exist before an affair, during an affair, and after an affair. It is in this examination process that the author invests her insights to contribute to the process of gathering information to help the reader process all of the possible circumstances, choices and consequences of an extra-marital affair. It is the original thoughts between the two extremes between the two walls that this book offers not to go too far. The whole dynamism is to do with all the factors pertaining to before the fact of an affair through the process of Beyond the Wedding Vows to after the fact of having an affair.

This book is an invitation to evaluate the overall significance of one's personal fulfillment as the basis of such a choice. In this case the author is not intending to take a moral stand about an affair. That is beyond the scope of the research. It is up to the individual, whether you have had an affair or are contemplating having one, to form an opinion or disseminate the information in *Beyond the Wedding Vows* according to one's own personal experiences, circumstances and needs, rather than becoming victims of your own choices.

CHAPTER ONE

What is Marriage?

"To marry unequally is to suffer equally."
Henri Frederic Amiel

*"Men like women with a past because they hope
history will repeat itself."*
Mae West

"I was married by a judge. I should have asked for a jury."
George Burns

MARRIAGE AT A GLANCE

Why do you think people marry? Love? Of course, love.
What other reason could there be? It is romantic to think
that people marry because they love each other so much
that they are willing to stand before country and God to
declare their feelings and solidify their commitment to one
another. All of us wish the happy couple well and genuinely hope that love will carry them through the turbulence we all know they will experience. But, in truth, love
sometimes has very little to do with marriage. Instead, it is
society and religion that play major roles in the institution
of marriage.

The history about the institution of marriage provides insight into how today's thoughts and customs about the institution have evolved. An understanding of the past provides us with ideas about our present and how our decisions are influenced. The customs and cultures regarding marriage in the past still reflect the mindset prevalent today.

Marriage was not designed as a legal institution for the union of a loving couple. Marriage was established to govern sexual behavior, and it is based on legal rights and religious doctrine. Ultimately, marriage was intended to bring families together, to protect and perpetuate property, money and position. According to the Biblical Hebraic version of Marriage in The Book of Numbers, where Moses gave the regulation regarding marriage to the Israelites, according to the instructions of the Lord, "They [daughters of Zelophehad] may marry anyone they please, provided they marry into a clan of their ancestral tribe, so that no heritage of the Israelites will pass from one tribe to another, but all the Israelites will retain their own ancestral heritage. Therefore, every daughter who inherits property in any of the Israelite tribes shall marry someone belonging to a clan of her own ancestral tribe, in order that all the Israelites may remain in possession of their own ancestral heritage. Thus, no heritage can pass from one tribe to another, but all the Israelite tribes will retain their own ancestral heritage" (Numbers 36:6-9).

Remember Romeo and Juliet? Apparently their union was not what their families had planned. Daughter Juliet did not obey her father's command to marry within the clan and suffered severe consequences.

Marriage evolved as an institution that controlled who would wed whom and who would be worthy of a particular family. It became a show of strength for those pursuing dowry, land, prestige and title. Love had nothing to do with it.

Enter organized religion. Producing offspring, reared in each person's particular religious traditions, to ensure the propagation of the faith, became the central role for married couples.

Because of the doctrine set forth by St. Augustine in about 400 AD, Christian leaders began to decree restricted guidelines for sexual conduct based on Christian thought and doctrine. Eventually marriage became sacred and divorce forbidden.

According to Lana Staheli, Ph.D, in her book *Triangles: Understanding, Preventing and Surviving an Affair,* Mohammed raised the status of Muslim women by requiring marriage between couples rather than allowing men to own women; men were expected to have as many as four wives. Japanese and Chinese men had concubines as well as wives. These women were required to be faithful to their husbands to protect the family lineage.

Staheli states, "In these early marriages, men took responsibility for women and children, but love wasn't part of the scenario." Augustus, in 17 BC, had this to say in a speech to support his own legislation encouraging marriage and childbearing: "If we could survive without a wife, citizens of Rome, all of us would do without that nuisance; but since nature has so decreed that we cannot manage comfortably with them, nor live in any way without them, we must plan for our lasting preservation rather than for our temporary pleasure." How many times have we heard many exasperated men proclaim, "Women, can't live with them, can't live without them!" Now we know where it came from and it is an example of how the mindset of today is still reflected in our past.

Cultures are known to have tolerated and adapted polygamy, polyandry and monogamy as ways of being married. Therefore, the meaning of the words "affair," "infidelity" and "adultery" will have different significance and definition with each given culture. For some, polygamy is considered bigamy or organized adultery, as portrayed by visiting foreigners to indigenous cultures. Fidelity was and, even today, is still not the standard among some cultures. For example, some cultures practice polygamy, where the husband is entitled to more than one wife. In our American culture, however, many people would consider this to be adultery.

Most people will agree that love and intimacy is not a prerequisite for making babies. Couples don't need affection or intimacy to procreate; they just need to have sex. Love has very little to do with marriage. It is determined by the family institution among all cultural societies. Obviously, today, in our culture, many people in love get married.

According to Staheli, "every culture and religion has its own history, values and traditions. Throughout history and without geographic boundaries, married people have had extra-marital affairs." In the final analysis, Staheli states, "No religious rule in the world has been successful in counteracting human sexual drives and eradicating infidelity." It's just human nature, pure and simple.

CULTURES AND ADULTERY

Women are persecuted more strongly than men are in all cultures that denounce adultery and sometimes are killed as a result. Anthropologist Suzanne Frayser of the University of Denver, author of *Varieties of Sexual Experience*, studied sexuality in sixty-two cultures, past and present, and found that in none of them do men experience a double standard. In other words, of those cultures that permitted adultery, not one allowed adultery for women and forbid it for men. In 26 percent of fifty-eight societies, the husband is allowed to have extra-marital sex, but not the wife. And of forty-eight societies for which Frayser had data, twenty-six, more than half, gave the husband the option to kill his unfaithful wife. Intrigued by the fact that, in these societies, illicit sex, mainly extra-marital sex, ranked only third in importance as grounds for divorce among men. Frayser says, "I realized that in many cases infidelity doesn't get to the point of litigation because the wife had been killed."

According to Dalma Heyn, in her book, *The Erotic Silence of the American Wife*, "Some societies simply define adultery differently for each gender. In Jewish Law, still on the books but varying from culture to culture, a married woman is guilty of adultery if she has sexual intercourse with any male other than her husband; a married man is guilty of adultery only if he has intercourse with another man's wife. Since the law allows polygamy for men (but not for women), it is reasoned that his affair with an unmarried woman might lead to his marrying her. It is neither "extra-marital" nor the "sex" of which the adulterous man is guilty, for it is neither his marriage nor his wife's honor he has legally violated. He has committed a property crime against another man."

Heyn further states, "Depending on the culture, an adulterous woman may be branded or speared in the leg or given over to any other men in the community who want to have sex with her. In the Senoufo and Bambara tribes of West Africa, such a woman is simply killed outright. Under Muslim law, too, a man may freely murder his wife if she is discovered having extra-marital sex. In modern Saudi Arabia, she could be stoned to death. In parts of Mexico she might have had her nose and ears cut off—before being stoned to death."

In their book *Sexual Arrangements: Marriage and the Temptation of Infidelity*, Janet Reibstein and Martin Richards describe the "marital ideal" as "not always been as it is today, nor is it the one exalted in non-Western cultures. Just a century ago marriage represented a coming together of families in property or possessions, an unequal partnership of a man and a woman in which the husband was the boss. It meant the joining of two people, perhaps in love, but not necessarily in intimate friendship and certainly not with expectations of equal sexual bliss. Over the past hundred years a new ideal has gradually evolved, one that encompasses most significantly the changes in women's roles, sexual experience, educational pursuits, and working lives. A companionate model that idealizes intimacy, support, and friendship and that demands a partnership of mutually satisfying sex has grown up."

Reibstein and Martin further contend that "just a century ago people did not live as long as they do now. Marriages then did not potentially span half a century. The ideal marriage is now that of the perfectly enriching partnership, endlessly satisfying. Over a short period this would be difficult enough. Over the longer lifetime of a marriage—often decades longer than our great-grandparents'—this is a very tall order, a greater demand on modern marriage."

MARRIAGE AS AN EVENT

Something Borrowed
Something Blue
Something Old
Something New

A woman told a story about a family reunion that she attended. She had been talking with her two nieces, whom she hadn't seen in several years. Susan was nineteen and Julie had just celebrated her twenty-first birthday and was about to graduate from college with highest honors. Both young women were articulate, intelligent and ...desperate to get married. The woman was curious about their point of view of marriage, especially since neither one was in a serious relationship. However, from their conversation, you would have thought that they were both engaged, with the wedding right around the corner. The girls described their rings, floral arrangements, and gowns in vast detail. Their mother was very happy that Susan had decided to wear her grandmother's wedding gown and chastised Julie for her decision to wear a shorter, more contemporary dress.

"Well," the mother said, "at least Julie has agreed to wear my pearls...that takes care of something borrowed."

The only thing that was missing in these beautiful planned weddings was a life-long partner who loved them and shared their dreams, goals and visions.

When asked to describe their ideal mate, they both laughed and said in unison, as though well rehearsed, "A guy who shows up for the wedding and has a nice butt." On a more serious note, they wanted a husband who provided well, wanted more than one child and did not spend too much time with his buddies. Love was never in the equation.

The "marriage event" has its root deep in a woman's psyche. The seed is planted when little girls receive their first bride doll, then begins to sprout and grow roots when she begins dressing up as a bride and playing house.

We can all imagine our families or friends sharing these scenarios. They are just another example of how our society today is still influenced by past ideologies that have been hard-wired into the psyche and very being of our society. Even in our post feminist era, many women still expect men to rescue and take care of them.

Perhaps this is the reason why some women ultimately become disillusioned and seek fulfillment outside of their marriage in an extra-marital affair. They are seeking to satisfy traditional societal roles, but eventually get caught in their own web of deceit. Does society do an injustice to our daughters by pressuring them to marry off their daughters to a family or man who can provide a better life for them and their children?

SUPERFICIAL INTIMACY

Let's imagine that Julie becomes engaged to Philip and they are planning to be married. They are "in love." When they are together they cling to each other and most of their time is spent together. They excite each other to the max! When they are together, heaven and earth collide. Their parents are extremely proud that they have both finally decided to "tie the knot." Everyone in both families is excited and preoccupied with the wedding plans.

How refreshing and gratifying this feels to their friends and family who realize that this wonderful feeling will not last. This is romantic love, we all know that it is quick to come and quick to go. Unless Julie and Philip develop the necessary skills of caring, discipline and attentiveness to survive a lifetime, it will not be surprising if they do not sustain their marriage vows when the romantic love ceases to exist.

Julie must be aware of Philip's resourcefulness and ambition to provide her with the type of lifestyle to which she is accustomed. She should discuss, in advance of her marriage, who will be responsible for raising their children. Julie must realize that, it is the woman generally, who gives up her independence for her children. She needs to ask herself just how independent she wants to remain. In short, does our society adequately prepare people who plan to marry?

We give our children years and years of lessons on everything from piano to soccer, but what about tips on a successful marriage? When we plan to marry we must consider and understand all of the ramifications of our choice. Couples need to know and understand why they have selected each other. Their relationship must provide intimacy, support and friendship above all else because they are essential to success in a marriage. They need to consider the influences of age, socioeconomic status, race, previous marital status and the educational level of their mate on their marriage. The "happy couple" must realize the ramifications and the likelihood of success in a marriage if these uncertainties are not addressed.

From all indications, Julie and Philip are surrendering to cultural and social demands. True, Julie's dad did not choose Philip and his family because they were the wealthiest tribe with the most land in the area, and Philip's parents didn't demand that Julie provide them with a sizeable dowry. But, all young people experience pressure to marry from cultural and social stereotyping. Julie and Philip are no exception.

Wedding celebrations today reflect the many cultural and social stereotypical traditions that couples include in their wedding plans. For example, Jewish wedding ceremonies take place under the chuppah, or wedding canopy, with two glasses and a bottle of kiddish wine. Italian wedding traditions are still prevalent, such as the bride assembling a trousseau before the ceremony, to bring to the marriage, and she is given a wedding shower to help her begin her married life. Additionally, she carries a *la borsa*, which is a small satin bag, in which guests place envelopes containing money to help the newly married couple begin their lives together. Most ethnic wedding celebrations include dancing and feasting after the wedding ceremony, which is a result of tradition that has been passed on from generation to generation. Ethnic ceremonies are influenced in some way by traditions that have been handed down through cultures and stereotypes.

The long history of romantic love still influences people in their decisions to marry. Couples practice many rituals to woo their potential mates. These rituals have been handed down throughout history. They can be as elaborate as lavish gifts or simple, like a love letter or flowers, but these rituals have emerged from many customs and are an important part of the courtship process.

It seems today that our daughters are desperate to marry. They seem to be trying to live up to cultural expectations and guidelines that have evolved throughout the ages. This is a superficial way to approach marriage, but none the less it still exists. As women we must begin to question this cultural phenomenon if we expect to guide our daughters and sons to embark on a well-thought-out plan for any consideration of marriage.

A SHIFTING REALITY

In 1973 a "how-to" guide for women who desired happy marriages, *The Total Woman*, by Marabel Morgan, hit the bookstands and talkshows. Those who feared feminism and the sexual revolution of the sixties readily embraced her ideas. Once again marriage fell prey to the traditional rules of church and state, where it has comfortably remained, until recently. Morgan promoted the following ideas: that women should adapt (regardless of her own wishes) the ways of her husband, who will reward her with "goodies;" that the husband, who the author calls a "king," makes all the final decisions and that the woman should not nag her "king." After all, according to Morgan, a secure woman will enjoy meeting her husband's needs.

The author's ideas reflected society's thoughts on what society accepted and what it rejected. Both men, and particularly women, bought into the concept that "out there" existed a total woman who was made whole by serving her husband's needs.

But it did not work. Women served, but found they were no more liberated by "The Total Woman" concept than they were by the freedom of the sixties. In fact, as time went on, the woman's liberation movement brought on a deeper understanding of what women were capable of accomplishing in the marketplace. This resulted in women and men redefining their world and their relationship to each other.

Choices for women expanded in the eighties and the concept of the superwoman evolved. Women, still searching for their own identity, bought into the I can do it and have it all concept, hook, line and sinker. Mostly, women sank because they had no role model.

In the nineties, the economic power of women forced both women and men into the awareness of their own and each other's limitations. They are not yet comfortable with this new awareness, but it has caused them to be less judgmental with each other's failings and to accept their own "sins" as opportunities to gain insight, which has lead to spiritual, emotional and psychological growth in the new millennium.

Today, this personal growth is causing society as a whole to be less judgmental. For the first time we are discovering the true meaning of the saying, "Except for the grace of God, there go I." We are more tolerant as a people.

What does this have to do with making a choice to have an extra-marital affair? Just this: That we as individuals choose how to live our lives—not the government, not the church, not society. In making a choice, we are the ones who will rejoice in the rewards or suffer the pains of our decisions. In other words, we alone must accept responsibility for our actions.

Our world is consistently changing its views regarding marriage, divorce and infidelity. At times we adopted a don't-ask-don't-tell policy; sometimes sex was viewed as a private affair; at other times it was held up to public scrutiny. What has not changed is that the individual must live by and answer her conscience alone by herself.

If there are consequences, for having an affair,—and there will be—the individual parties involved must be prepared to pay the price. They may lose their children; their marriage may end; they may suffer financially, and their social status may be deeply affected. In many cases, all of the above may happen.

Before becoming involved with someone outside of marriage, do yourself a favor and take the time to ask yourself some very important questions. Then listen carefully to the answers. This process may save you a lot of soul-searching and pain after the fact.

CHAPTER TWO

What's Lacking Within?

"Women give sex to get love and men give love to get sex."
Unknown

"Marriage is a great institution, but I'm not ready for an institution."
Mae West

"The trouble with some women is that they get all excited about nothing—and then marry him."
Cher

RETHINKING YOUR COMMITMENT

People are basically in search of happiness in one form or another. It is essential for their well being and peace of mind to come to a workable alternative or balance, when deciding which course to pursue when engaged in an extra-marital affair that will enhance their life and possibly their marriage. Usually people are not equipped to handle conflicts or other situations that arise from infidelity, which leads to unhappy consequences.

One does not enter into an intimate marriage contract with the intention of having an affair with another person. We enter marriage with high aspirations, intent on achieving mutual goals. However, there are countless situations and circumstances that have led married women to undertake affairs. Let's talk in terms of you, specifically.

Going beyond the original commitment of your marriage contract and having an extra-marital affair will cause you to rethink your commitment and ask yourself why you find the need to look elsewhere. Perhaps you are responding to and trying to compensate for something that is unsatisfactory, incomplete or inadequate in your married relationship. On the other hand, many people are trying to compensate for inadequacies in their own personalities.

PINPOINT YOUR DEFICIENCIES

Let's assume that you have already met someone to whom you are attracted and you have made up your mind that you want to have an affair with him. For the moment, put aside the question of why you are physically attracted to him, ignore the butterflies of longing and desire fluttering in your stomach. Clear your mind of all distractions and focus on the following questions.

What is lacking in your life? This is a key question that will help identify long lost dreams, ambitions and desires. This is not an easy question to answer because it forces you to come face to face with who you once were, who you are now, and who you want to become. Once all of that is on the table, you have to make a choice. Which dreams are still worth pursuing? Maybe you are not satisfied with your current career and you want to pursue greater financial independence. You understand that this will mean that you will need to go back to school, but you feel that you do not have the energy to see this come to fruition. Maybe you have wanted to begin working after being at home raising children and you want to finish your college education first.

Perhaps you have wanted to relocate your family to another area that you perceive is more desirable. Your logic is that the move will revitalize your mind, but your husband cannot leave his current job. Maybe these dreams are affecting your decision to have an extra-marital affair because you feel that the affair would pacify these dreams and provide a compromise for you to bolster your self-esteem.

Do you lack intellectual stimulation? Maybe you are seeking spiritual fulfillment and have the idea that you will soon discover your soul mate. Once this discovery is made you believe that you will be complete. Does completeness come only through another person? Can you be complete on your own? Does completeness mean that you will be happy forever? Are there degrees of completeness?

Are your needs physical? In this case you need to ask yourself what you are lacking in terms of physical expression in your marriage. This question may lead to the discovery that you have latent sexual desires that you may find frightening or repulsive.

It is obvious that either something in your marriage is deficient or something in your personality is lacking when you elect to pursue an extra-marital affair. Perhaps, for instance, honesty is important to you. Will you be able to sustain an affair knowing that what you have chosen is not honest? Once you realize what you want in a relationship and that what you want is lacking in your current marriage, you will be able to pool your resources and identify your fears, hates and desires. Realizing what you hope for and believe in, and what you are committed to and value, will equip you with the confidence to make the right choice: a choice that will benefit you.

MAKE A HEALTHY EMOTIONAL ASSESSMENT

When we conduct a frank and healthy assessment of our emotions, we can truly know ourselves and find inner peace. Be aware of your emotions and pay attention to your emotional reactions. Ask yourself what you are feeling. Do you feel embarrassment if you are not living up to your or your husband's expectations? Do you fear someone or something?

Admit your emotions. Turn your full awareness toward these emotions. Estimate, too, how strong each one is. Do you feel angry? Is your desire to have an affair your attempt to rebel against cultural stereotyping, or are you affirming your desire to connect with someone who is intellectually on a par with you?

Investigate your emotions, including anger. Ask your anger how it got there and where it came from. Trace the origin of your emotions. You may just get a glimpse of an inferiority complex to which you have never admitted.

Sheri, a bright, effusive thirty-six year old attorney, married to Martin for seven years, decided that she wanted to become a partner in the law firm where she worked. There were no other women partners in the firm and this angered her. She was willing to sacrifice the time she cherished at home with her four-year-old daughter to put in the necessary hours to realize her dream of partnership. She worked seventy and eighty hours a week and traveled extensively for nearly two years. The opportunity to become a partner never materialized.

This disappointment crushed her spirit to persevere and continue her effort to realize her dream of partnership in her law firm and her lack of tenacity angered her. Additionally, she lost the time with her daughter that she could never recover, and this added to her frustration. She eventually left that firm and began working from home on different legal consulting projects. Joseph contracted her to help his firm negotiate several legal contracts. Sheri was physically attracted to Joseph and this led to an intense affair. Joseph had been married for twelve years, he had two small children. His wife discovered his infidelity and took her frustration out directly on Sheri, by slashing Sheri's car tires and smashing her office window. Joseph's wife obtained the list of some of Sheri's clients, she began calling them to inform them that Sheri was an adulteress. It was an ugly nightmare for Sheri. She broke off the affair with Joseph. Sheri's husband found out, but he told her that despite her betrayal he still loved her and wanted to remain in the marriage. He encouraged Sheri to seek professional counseling and both of them decided to work with a marriage counselor.

In counseling, Sheri learned that she had never resolved the crisis and scars from the disappointment of the law firm. She had a tremendous amount of anger and she reacted with the affair before she resolved these conflicts. She felt guilty for affecting Joseph's marriage and deceiving Martin, and had to come to grips with that guilt. It only created more inner chaos and confusion. Coming to terms with her choice, to react instead of settling her disappointment, only created dire consequences. Sheri learned that she felt inferior to her male counterparts in the law firm and this deficiency blocked her from realizing professional success.

A marriage that lacks shared and mature love, results in an effort to fulfill basic emotional needs. Satisfying your self-esteem needs helps you to be more confident, strong and capable. Feeling secure and stable in your marriage fulfills your need to be safe and giving, and receiving affection helps you to feel loved. When we desire to fulfill these needs outside of the marriage contract, we create inner turmoil, which effects our balance and interferes with the roles we play within the structure of marriage.

Perhaps you are seeking affirmation that you are attractive and important. Do you want to confirm that you are capable of being accepted and wanted by another person? Knowing yourself and what you wish to gain is all-important in averting an affair or beginning one.

Anita's marriage to Gordon wasn't measuring up to her expectations of what she imagined a good marriage to be. She rationalized that Gordon should allow time with her to share intimate evenings out to dinner and frequent vacations separate from their two small children, that they should allot time for each other on a weekly basis, and that Gordon should not go out with his friends on Tuesdays to bowl. Although their finances would not support the extra expense of dinners and vacations, she still insisted that Gordon comply with her wishes. She became relentless to this end and fought with Gordon every day. Gordon's position was that they possibly could compromise with one short weekend vacation each year and maybe eating out once a month. This did not appease Anita. She truly believed that these demands were not frivolous or unreasonable but essential to fulfill her basic emotional needs to relate with Gordon, like, she thought, mature married people relate. Anita's next door neighbor, Ted, stayed home with his children and his wife worked. Eventually, Anita and Ted had an affair. Anita's four-year old son told his daddy that Mr. Ted was sleeping on daddy's side of the bed, and when the four-year-old had to take a nap he didn't like sharing his bedroom with the neighbor children.

Anita's husband wasn't amused and he demanded a divorce. It was only after two years of counseling that Anita realized that she was being immature and that the demands she was making on Gordon, were made to fulfill her need to feel accepted and wanted by her husband. Additionally, she viewed getting away with her husband as the only way to have fun in her marriage. She didn't know how to create a relationship based on caring and true friendship. Anita, unrealistically, believed that Ted would fulfill these needs in some sort of romantic fashion. It was because of this misdirected choice that she created a great deal of inner turmoil for herself and upheaval for her son and husband. The role Anita interpreted her husband should play, to be the proper husband, interfered with the reality that went above and beyond realistic expectations. Gordon refused to make these extraordinary efforts to please Anita and she felt it necessary to go outside of her marriage for fulfillment.

If you desire to be intimate with or get to know another person who is not your spouse, you may experience an undulating wave of emotions. To help you through this tremor, it is necessary to go through a process where you try to learn if you are compatible with each other or if you are mature enough to handle an extra-marital affair. The risks that you are taking are great, analyzing and assessing the situation ahead of time can help you alleviate problems in the future. Begin by gathering information about the person to whom you are attracted and try to gain more knowledge about him. Create opportunities to spend time with him and begin to try to find his best qualities. The attraction to these qualities presents you with a challenge. Ask yourself, "What do the qualities that I admire in this person, who is not my spouse, fulfill in my own personal spectrum of needs?" When you begin to wish to possess and desire this person, the thoughts for an affair begin. You can proceed to act with caution, or you may decide that you do not need to fill any void, that your relationship with your spouse is sufficient. Your desire for the other person may be a chemical attraction that has worn off before you can act on it.

Sue Larkin had been married for twelve years, to a man who truly loved her and whom she truly loved. Sue was a creative woman with many ideas and a great deal of ambition. She always saw herself as, if not special, then different. She felt she had a lot to contribute to the world. But for all of her marriage, she worked at jobs that held little interest to her. She kept telling herself and her husband that as soon as things were in order with his job, their house and their finances, it would be her turn to spread her wings.

Her husband agreed and encouraged her to fulfill her dreams.

Sue enrolled in a prestigious art program that required her to commute four hours round trip. She found the trip enjoyable because it gave her time to think. A few weeks into the course, she began to develop an intellectual relationship with George, her instructor, who was approximately her age. Their initial conversations focused on the subject of painting and he began to coach her on what he perceived were the weak points in her work. Up until that time, the only feedback she had received was her husband's high approval of anything she painted, no matter how inadequate she thought it was.

Soon Sue and George's conversations turned personal. A cup of coffee turned into having dinner, and walks around the campus became trips to museums. Because of their shared interests, Sue justified her eventual love affair with George as "something that was destined to happen."

When the affair ended and Sue confessed it to her husband, "destiny" sounded like a feeble excuse, even to Sue. She realized, for the first time, that she risked everything, her husband, her home and her integrity. Then she began to ask herself why she really had the affair in the first place.

One wound that was opened for Sue was discovering what her definition of love was. Sue's interpretation of love was helping someone develop through criticism, like her mother gave her, not growing through nurturing acceptance, like her husband offered her. This awakening led Sue to change her entire life. She no longer accepted loving and being loved in what Sue called the "wrong" way. For the first time in her life, Sue felt she had come to understand how good the "right" kind of love could be. This unfolding took Sue years to accomplish.

Maybe if Sue would have done some fact-finding, asking herself realistically and honestly what she was lacking in the first place, she could have saved herself a lot of pain and the loss of inner peace. Perhaps she would have decided that her husband was her "right" love in the first place.

EMOTIONAL MATURITY

Escaping from your marital relationship because of a conflicted marriage, emotional immaturity, like Anita, or neuroses, are the leading causes of extra-marital affairs. But what characteristics does the "perfect" couple possess? There are many exhausting studies and psychological evaluations on the ideal mature couple and relationship.

To summarize many different interpretations, including those of Sigmund Freud and Abraham Maslow, the ideal emotionally mature couple is characterized by Herbert S. Strean, in his book *The Extramarital Affair*, in the following ways:

> The two members of this partnership receive much pleasure and fulfillment from relating mutually with each other.
>
> They enjoy each other in a mutually trusting, intimate, and devoted relationship.
>
> They can trust each other without feeling guilty about being dependent.
>
> They have a sense of their own identities and can take care of themselves if the other person is not available.
>
> They can enjoy feeling independent without resentment because they have a realistic sense of their own strengths and limitations.
>
> They are not busy doubting one another.
>
> They can love and enjoy each other sexually without making excessive demands or seeking codependence.
>
> They can admire each other without being infatuated and can enjoy intimacy and mutual devotion without swallowing each other up or fearing that they will be swallowed up in the process.
>
> They lack nothing physically or emotionally from their relationship.

In short they are both emotionally mature.

Engaging in an extra-marital affair causes you to rethink your commitment to your marriage and set sail on a wave of soul-searching and questioning. You begin to look into your own short-comings by examining inside of yourself, searching for possible deficiencies or personality flaws, trying to understand if you are compensating for your own inadequacies. You scrutinize what you hope to achieve and what you hold the most value in, and exactly what it is you are committed to. You become aware of your emotions and your reactions, and finally, you question the compatibility and qualities of the man for which you may give up your marriage. In giving due diligence, you will be confident that you are making the right choice.

CHAPTER THREE

Robb, Steale and Cheatham?

"A thing worth having is a thing worth cheating for."
W.C. Fields

"Honesty has ruined more marriages than infidelity."
Charles McCabe

REALIZING THE HARMFUL EFFECTS

You may not think that you are robbing, stealing from, or cheating yourself or anyone else, when you have an extra-marital affair, but in actuality you are. Sadly, the main "beneficiary" of this deceit is you. Additionally, until you make a decision, you are paying consequences that cannot be measured in financial or temporal loss. The result will be consequences that you will pay in terms of your emotions, your health, your time, your character and your values. All of these valuable assets in your life will be compromised. Your emotions go on a roller coaster ride, your health is negatively affected and you jeopardize your self-esteem and self-respect. You are gambling with your financial future as well as your mental and physical health.

An extra-marital affair will cause you much grief and anguish. The trouble may begin because your marriage is making you emotionally and physically ill, or, it can be a result of the coping strategies that you are facing, because of the affair, that is causing you to be off balance. You must make an assessment of the costs you will pay and decide if the consequences are worth the cost.

The people affected by your decisions are, usually the most important people in your life—your children and your husband, and they must also be taken into consideration. What consequences will they face? If you have an affair, do not practice safe sex and as a result contract a sexually transmitted disease such as genital herpes or AIDS, your husband will be at risk. You may compromise the health of your family for your own gratification.

Intuitively, you may have long suspected that you are not yourself mentally or physically. You seem to have lost your edge and are unsure of where you are going. You probably haven't realized how much this conflict is taking a toll on your mental and physical health.

When you involve yourself in an extra-marital affair, you allow yourself to become intimate with and vulnerable to your forbidden partner. This is why the damage potential is great. Not only are you risking your own physical or mental well-being, you are also threatening your family's welfare. In her book *Lethal Lovers and Poisonous People: How to Protect Your Health from Relationships that Make You Sick*, Harriet B. Braiker, Ph.D., cites seven "deadly signs of a toxic relationship." Five of those signs become evident when you are involved in an extra-marital affair. If you find yourself experiencing helplessness, anxiety, conflict, loss of self-esteem or frustration, perhaps you should re-evaluate your lifestyle. You will find that all of these woes are now a part of your life and that you are paying for the choices you have made.

HELPLESSNESS

When you experience helplessness you become vulnerable and dependent. You cannot act without help from someone or something, because you are too confused and weak to act independently. You become out of control and are unable to cope with ordinary stresses of life, such as the multiple demands made on mothers, like car-pools, homework, meals, *et cetera,* that usually demand your attention concurrently. Braiker contends that eating, drinking, smoking or exercising excessively, or having frequent temper tantrums or crying for no apparent reason are also signs of helplessness. Perhaps you lack the capability to focus or concentrate. You feel crushed by everyday occurrences, such as a child's thoughtless remark or an inability to fix a balky appliance. You begin to feel ambushed, as if you have no alternative but continue to go on, feeling overwhelmed and incompetent. You can't make yourself feel better. In trying to break out of this feeling, you may find yourself sleeping too much or using drugs or alcohol to deaden the pain of being suffocated by your problems. These coping mechanisms are both futile and self-destructive; they will make you to feel even worse. Eventually, you will become depressed.

Additionally, according to Harriet B. Braiker, Ph.D., "prolonged feelings of hopelessness activate excessive secretions of the stress hormone cortisol, interfering with your immune system's ability to fight bacteria, viruses, and environmental toxins, and to screen out renegade cells that might develop into cancer. Feeling overwhelmed and out of control can present particularly serious risks if you already have an underlying vulnerability to autoimmune diseases such as diabetes or rheumatoid arthritis. Finally, chronic helplessness can trigger a worrisome biochemical imbalance by depleting your brain's supply of a chemical called dopamine, a situation which produces symptoms of depression."

ANXIETY

Anxiety can be described as a nervous disorder characterized by a state of excessive uneasiness. Uncertainty, appre-
hensiveness and constant worry go along with anxiety.
Open up any dictionary and look up the words anxiety or
anxious and you will be appalled at the long list of troubling attributes that accompany them. Anxiety is destructive to your mental and physical well-being.

What causes you to feel anxious during an affair? Often
you do not know exactly where this affair will take your
life. You are always left feeling like everything is "up in the
air." It is difficult to see ahead and prepare for where the
relationship or your marriage is heading. As a result, you
become anxious.

If either relationship lacks encouragement, solidity and the
promise of continuation, the anxiety you experience is fu-
eled by fear that you will be left alone. When you or your
lover cannot promise each other fidelity, you become anxious because your future is left to chance. Anxiety exagger-
ates your feelings of stability and you begin to feel apprehensive and defenseless. You feel out of charge with your life.

According to Harriet B. Braiker, Ph.D., "Chronic feelings
of anxiety can damage your health in many ways. Protracted
anxiety depresses the function of your immune system's
natural killer cells designed to fight bacterial and viral in-
fections. Tension and nervousness often produce headaches
(including migraines), muscular and digestive disorders,
exacerbation of painful arthritic conditions, diabetes and
other immune or autoimmune diseases, numerous skin
disorders, and many other maladies."

Braiker further contends that anxiety is itself an emotional disorder and is closely related to depression. "Protracted anxiety, caused by an unpredictable, unstable, or
capricious relationship, triggers helplessness, loss of control, and clinical depression."

Finally, according to Braiker, anxiety can lead many people to engage in abusing alcohol or drugs to produce feelings of tranquility. This abuse will add further to that out-of-control feeling and depression.

CONFLICT

Conflict is, according to The Oxford Dictionary, "The clashing of opposed principles." Feeling that you don't want to remain in your marriage...that you cannot decide what will be better for you in the future...that you cannot find satisfaction in your affair...that you feel constantly torn because you are so uncertain of your loyalties, can make you hostile.

Everyone in your life becomes unsympathetic to what you are experiencing and you feel antagonized and disagreeable. Perhaps you often shout at your children and your husband or criticize them, saying cruel things because you always seem upset. Conflict between the life you wish you had and the reality you face leaves you feeling a great deal of hostility toward yourself and others.

Conflict and hostility are usual reactions to lack of fulfillment, deceit and cheating. Hostility manifests itself in combativeness and antagonistic outbursts. Hostility can be evident if you find yourself taking offense more often than usual or find yourself insulting your children and husband or using vulgar language more than you usually do. Hostility becomes apparent when you argue and quarrel more often with your husband and children because you have pent-up frustrations. Maybe you feel hostile or conflicted because your spouse is not loyal to you or you begin to feel guilty because you are betraying your basic values and family, or your new partner is not living up to your expectations. Whatever the case, the feeling of being conflicted frustrates you and you begin to act out against the very people who are most important in your life.

Harriet Braiker has much to say about conflict and hostility. She believes that they are "pernicious emotions that can wreak serious psychological and physical havoc on you and your partner. Hostility is the lethal quality most closely associated with heart and vascular disease in aggressive people. The mechanism through which hostility exerts its heavy toll is a build-in built-in, primitive stress reaction known as 'fight or flight.'"

According to Braiker, "too much hostility over a sustained period of time results in a heightened risk of heart attack and other cardiovascular disease. Furthermore, the constant stimulation of the potent fight-or-flight response can trigger a massive coronary artery spasm leading to a major, and potentially fatal, heart attack."

Constantly trying to keep the hostility and conflicted pain you feel inside can be damaging as well. "Over time, the long-suppressed anger eventually boils over and explodes," Braiker continues. You begin to "run the risk of breaking down a critical function of your immune system that screens renegade cells and you become vulnerable to diseases such as cancer, high cholesterol, AIDS, and a range of other infectious and contagious illnesses."

Melva, a forty-two year old with four children, found herself caught in an intense love affair with a man she met at her aerobics class. She was having a difficult time coping with the demands of the children, the house and her new lover. He, too, was very conflicted because he felt guilty for betraying his wife and child. Both of them commiserated together and had lengthy discussions about how they would remain in the affair and handle the guilt and demands at home. The passion was too strong to break off the affair. However, both of them continually argued with their spouses and Melva even hit her fourteen-year old daughter for talking back. She never hit any of her children. Melva even started to insult her husband in front of her children, something she never had done before. Aside from too many demands on her, Melva was having nightmares about her children and her lover's child. She developed asthma and a mysterious itching that became almost unbearable at night. It was only through professional counseling that Melva was able to realize that she did not love her husband and that she was strong enough to face the process of separation and divorce. She realized that she was better off divorced than living her life in constant chaos and upheaval.

Like Melva, many women experience this conflict and hostility while going through an extra-marital affair. It is important for your health and the welfare of your family that you recognize these symptoms to seek help. You must make an assessment of the consequences you are paying and determine if having an affair is worth the risk and make a choice that will not jeopardize your health, your well-being and your family.

LOSS OF SELF-ESTEEM

Self-esteem is having a good opinion of yourself and means you have self-confidence. It is vital for you to be a healthy and happy human being. Throughout your life, you have heard about the effects of the lack of self-esteem. You know or have heard that when people lack self-esteem they react to everything in their lives in a self-destructive manner, either because they feel they are being deprived of basic needs, or they feel that they do not measure up to society's expectations of them.

According to Worchel and Shebilske in their book *Psychology: Principles and Applications*, "self-esteem is very important because it determines how we act and how we perceive our world. Because self-esteem is so vital to the way we behave, it is crucial that it includes an honest representation of our feelings, values, and experiences, not just those that society or the people around us find 'acceptable.' "

Your self-esteem will begin to deteriorate if you realize that a life choice you made was not the best one for you. When you begin to feel unimportant, unappreciated, wronged, or inadequate in your marriage or relationship, your self-esteem begins to crumble. As a result, you start to question your choice. Your confidence is eroded because you know you have made a mistake.

If you begin to feel inferior and deficient regarding your self-image, and pessimistic in how you view yourself, and your self-confidence and self-respect are decreasing, you are experiencing a loss of self-esteem. Braiker states that "loss of self-esteem is closely related to each of the other deadly signs and, consequently, poses similar risks to your physical health. And by definition, it is emotionally injurious, since positive, solid self-esteem is deemed a core criterion of good mental health."

FRUSTRATION

When you cannot achieve a purpose or believe that you are unfulfilled because your needs in many areas are lacking, you ultimately become frustrated. You begin to feel ineffective and discontent. The more you endure this dissatisfaction, the more frustrated you become, and this will manifest itself in many characteristics.

Braiker maintains that "continual frustration of your significant needs invariably will generate feelings of anger, resentment, and, eventually, outrage. Despite attempts to control, deny, or rationalize your ire, it eventually will be aroused if your partner (or the relationship) fails to satisfy your needs for affection, sex, attention, acceptance, approval, reassurance, praise, or any other emotional requirements. Poor communication can be a major source of frustration—and eventually hostility—in relationships. When communication breaks down, your ability to discuss and resolve your problems is impaired. As a result, your relationship may be plagued by repetitive cycles of conflict over the same issues, causing further feelings of helplessness and futility. Hostility leads back to frustration and a dangerous cycle is established."

If you continue to suppress this hostility, you will become frustrated. If you cannot vent your frustrations, you will become even more depressed and possibly experience serious physical afflictions.

There are many examples and case studies of the harmful effects of being off balance in your life, when you are in a relationship with which you are unhappy. Women act out their heartache and sadness by exhibiting behavior that ranges from using vulgar language to even physically hurting their spouses and children. The toll on their physical and mental health, goes beyond economic or temporal loss.

SO WHY DO IT?

The inevitable question remains: "Why do it?" Why do so many people continue extra-marital affairs? Why do so many people continue to stay in unhealthy marriages? In either situation, you experience detrimental effects to your emotional and physical health and you become half the person you have been; yet you perpetuate your own suffering.

Despite all the negative effects, that many people engaged in an extra-marital affair experience, affairs are common. People believe they benefit from affairs, even though they may also suffer from them.

There are powerful incentives to participate in affairs, even though they may be illicit or immoral for some, and charged with feelings of guilt for others. Despite all the admonitions of "Don't do it!" from peers and society, affairs have become a common part of everyday life for many.

People believe that affairs bring excitement and stimulation into their lives. In the beginning, they feel increased self-esteem and sexual attractiveness. They are satisfied by the sexual and emotional pleasure of their affair and often have expectations of nothing more. There are problems and conflicts, as in other relationships, but most lovers, while the affair lasts, feel that the benefits outweigh the pain. Even afterward, looking back, most feel they have gained from the affair.

CHAPTER FOUR

Are You Willing to Question Your Morals and Ethics?

"In order to preserve your self-respect, it is sometimes necessary to lie and cheat."
Robert Byrne

"It has been my experience that folks who have no vices have very few virtues."
Abraham Lincoln

"Oh Lord, help me to be pure, but not yet."
St. Augustine

"Living with a conscience is like driving a car with the brakes on."
Budd Schulberg

VALUE CHECK

We act morally to avoid punishment, to gain praise, to attain happiness, to be dignified, or to fit in with society. We should do to others what we would want others to do to us. Using this same reasoning, we believe that it is wrong to lie, to harass, victimize, assault, or kill others. And let us not forget the fundamental principals that govern all of us in America, which are the rights to life, liberty and happiness.

In a traditional sense, being a morally and ethically good person means that we follow precisely defined rules of conduct set forth in The Ten Commandments, such as "don't kill," or "don't steal." Presumably, we must learn these rules, and then make sure each of our actions live up to the rules.

Plato emphasized four virtues in particular, which were later called cardinal virtues: wisdom, courage, temperance and justice. Other important virtues are fortitude, generosity, self-respect, good temper, and sincerity. Perhaps our parents stressed the importance of developing good habits of character, such as goodwill. Once I've acquired goodwill, for example, I will then habitually act in a charitable manner. In addition to advocating good habits of character, our parents might have warned us to avoid negative character traits, or vices, such as cowardice, insensibility, injustice and vanity.

When we are faced with difficult decisions do we ask ourselves what is "the best thing to do?" Do you believe your decisions are based more on what society expects you to do, or what you would feel is best for your?

Do you ask yourself what the best course of action would be to pursue? Aristotle held that we use reason to determine the best way to achieve the highest moral good. He saw virtues as good habits that we acquire, which regulate our emotions. For example, when you fear something, you should develop the virtue of courage to allow yourself to be firm when you face danger.

As human beings we have clear obligations, such as to care for our children and not to commit murder. Obligations become our duties. We have duties to ourselves, which include self-improvement, such as educating ourselves, and we have duties to our families, which include honoring our parents. Lastly, we have social duties, which include keeping promises and not harming others.

Happiness is feeling pleasure and contentment and the success of all that you work for, such as well-adjusted children, education, or an accomplishment such as building a business is enjoyed. All people strive for happiness, and moral reasoning involves determining the best means for achieving that end. For example, if your happiness is attained by being courageous and stopping an affair from happening or being courageous and going ahead with an affair, then your reason will tell you what actions you need to perform to be courageous, that is, avoiding both cowardly and rash behavior.

EVALUATING THE CONSEQUENCES

Consequences are different for everyone's different circumstances. For example, if extra-marital affairs involve children the consequences will be different from the consequences of the woman who has no children. Consequences can be positive and consequences can be negative. Additionally, your actions may have unintended consequences. For instance, you may begin an affair impulsively and realize that it was a mistake but you become pregnant and are caught with consequences that are long lasting. However, individual consequences can be limited if we realize the extent to which we will be impacted either positively or negatively.

Aside from different circumstances determining the outcome of your choice and negative, positive or unintended consequences, the process that you undergo to resolve your dilemma is important. When faced with an extra-marital affair, you begin to weigh the consequences of your actions and call upon your reasoning and your character, as well as your morals and ethics to guide you in making a decision. If you are trying to come to grips with the idea of having an extra-marital affair and are contemplating what you should or should not do, try to take a realistic assessment of your particular situation. For example, if you decide to pursue an affair, will you leave your husband or will you realize that what you have done is a mistake. Good or bad, you will have consequences.

Keep in mind that you are not alone and that many people have difficulty accepting that their actions have consequences and that they are responsible for their actions. If you are involved in an affair, this process of evaluating the consequences you may face will help you to focus on your specific circumstances. Try to put your emotions on hold and look at your situation through the eyes of your husband and children and what consequences they will be facing. We often seek to blame what has been done to us as an excuse for bad behavior. Some people are forced to overcome greater difficulties than others do, yet we each choose the attitude with which we approach life and the actions we take. We are not programmed like a computer. We are not helpless puppets of a vindictive puppeteer. As theologians tell us, we are born with free will, the ability to choose our own paths.

To make a wise decision, we must take inventory of the good and bad consequences of our actions, and add up the pleasure and pain that will result from our actions. It is important that we realize and take into consideration how others will be affected. Others include your children or your lover's children or your lover's wife or your husband. In making this decision, we must determine whether the good consequences outweigh the bad. When the good consequences are higher, then we believe we can make the "right" decision.

If you decide to have an affair and you do not have children and your lover does not have children or a wife then your choice will have less of an affect than if you have children and your lover has children, because fewer lives will be changed. Your choice to have an affair will impact only you and your husband. If you have children and your lover is married with children then your choice will obviously impact more people. The complexity of the consequences will touch more or less people depending on your situation.

Many times our decisions are based on moral rules. Most people believe moral rules protect us from other self-centered people. Our property, our families, and even our lives are at continual risk. To ensure civilized communities, we embrace a basic set of rules that encourages people to consider others as well as themselves.

WEIGHING THE FACTS

Relying on blind intuition, that is, not thinking through the issue of whether or not you should pursue an extra-marital affair, can result in far-reaching consequences. By gathering the facts of consequences such as the loss of custody of your children or substantial loss of income, we can be better readied to act responsibly. Take into consideration your own self-interest, your pleasure, the law and your religion.

Having a set of rules or a code of ethics that you live by helps you understand your direction. For instance, perhaps you never allow yourself to talk about a valued friend or you always make it a point to have compassion on the people who are less fortunate than yourself, by sacrificing in order that you can give them a portion of your income. Lying is another character trait that you must consider. Some people believe that their character is weak if they lie and many people believe that lying is wrong no matter what the circumstances. Although many people never intend to lie, having an extra-marital affair will involve lying to your spouse. You must question values regarding your position on extra-marital sex and monogamy. Having an extra-marital affair will obligate you to engage in questionable behavior that will cause you to judge the worth of your actions as well as your values and rules, which you live according to. Codes of ethics that you might believe are morally right and genuine and principled in customs and societal standards as well as religious beliefs. Your code of ethics helps give you direction and order in your life.

MORAL DILEMMA

Being moral is being concerned with the goodness or bad-
ness of human character or behavior, or with the distinc-
tion between right and wrong; concerned with accepted
rules and standards of human behavior; conforming to accepted standards of general conduct.

A moral dilemma involves a situation in which a person has
only two courses of action available, each of which requires
performing a morally impermissible action. For example, a
person in an abusive marriage might face the dilemma of staying in the marriage and taking the abuse or starting an affair. In
other words, a moral dilemma is a situation in which, if you
carry out an obligation, you will be responsible for an outcome
you do not wish to create. For example, you support free speech,
but you don't want to support a Neo-Nazi march in a Jewish
neighborhood because you don't want to insult and infuriate
the Jewish Community. What do you do?

When you make eye contact with a person who gives
you goosebumps, and when you have a very strong urge to
flirt with that person, do your morals take over, do you
cease to feel "turned on?"

If you haven't questioned yourself about your beliefs regarding the above questions, you certainly will if you find
yourself having an affair or thinking about having an affair.
Furthermore, questioning your moral or ethical code will
help you to find a "center" and foundation that will help to
protect your self-respect and self-esteem. You cannot tinker
with ethics. Questioning one's own morals or ethics ought
to undermine the foundation on which you built your life
and will weaken or destroy your self-respect. Changing one's
morals is a cataclysmic event.

LOST IN SPACE: DUTIES VERSUS SELF

A duty is a moral obligation that you have to another person, such as the duty not to lie. Some people believe that

duties are obligations from others that are "due" them. Do you believe that your relationship has certain rights that are due you because of the marriage contract? Does your spouse believe this? According to this view, every right that I have implies a duty on your part to respect my right. For example, married couples have the duty not to have extramarital sex. However, some people believe that their duties or obligations toward preserving the marriage contract are more important than rights. Many women have decided that, because of the negative stigma of divorce, their religious beliefs, or the harmful effects of divorce on children, will not divorce and thus endure a painful existence. They believe that their duty to preserve the marriage contract is more important than their own peace of mind and well-being.

Millie, a devout Catholic from an ethnic family with three children, found herself in this very predicament. Her husband, John, gambled away all of his pay checks and had affairs with a string of women throughout their marriage. She worked two jobs and cared for the children. The children accepted this "arrangement" as a typical life situation, although they experienced many hardships, such as women constantly showing up on their front porch and asking for "Johnny" only to realize that he was a married man with three children. Utility men always coming to the house to shut-off the gas and electric, was a common occurrence. The worst of their experiences was the fact that Millie was always very hostile. One time Millie even held the family at gunpoint threatening to kill John in the presence of the children. The smallest child was able to escape and seek the help of a neighbor and the police were summoned to the rescue. No one was hurt and Millie wasn't carted off to the police station, but the incident left indelible marks on her children. Millie lived this lifestyle for more than forty-three years and when her husband died, her children encouraged her to seek counseling. She realized after all of this grief that she was frightened to be a single mother and wasn't secure enough or confident in herself that she would be able to make it on her own. Fortunately, her children supported and encouraged her. Her greatest victory is that her children have been able to live successful productive lives. Millie would never have imagined divorcing her husband because of the negative social connotations of divorce and the effects she believed that divorce would have had on her children.

What happens when a couple's circumstances change? When a conflict arises, such as spousal abuse, and it isn't in the best interest of one spouse; does it remain her duty to observe the duties of the marriage contract? Perhaps, most people believe, Millie would have found some peace if she could have escaped from her miserable existence with a man who really cared for her, and engaged in an extra-marital affair. Since her convictions were so strong against divorce she would have had some semblance of sanity for her own well-being and peace of mind, instead of constantly having temper tantrums and constantly screaming at her children. Conflict arises when we must choose between duties to others or duties to ourselves. Do we then reflect back upon our moral convictions?

Do we consider the duties of self-preservation or self-improvement above the duty to remain faithful to a spouse that is not living up to his end of the marriage contract? Do we have a priority? Is an affair the only way to address the conflict? There is no clear set of guidelines that we will be able to draw upon, and that in and of itself is a conflict.

What about benefits? Do our choices have benefits or what are the beneficial consequences of our decisions? Millie's children still had the presence of their father and were able to get financial help from their father's mother to afford a parochial education. This benefit would not have been available to them if Millie divorced John, because

John's mother made it clear that she would not help support Millie's children if she divorced.

Take the case of Christine, a thirty-three year old mother of two children. She has been married to Kevin, an oral surgeon, for nine years. Kevin has been unfaithful to Christine in the past, but they have always been able to overcome the trauma to their marriage and reconcile. Something happened that changed her life. By chance, Christine was reading the divorce decrees in the newspaper one morning when she saw the notice of the divorce of her high school sweetheart. Matt and Christine had been very close in high school and had dated for two years. Sexual tension between the two became the focus of their relationship because Christine would not give in to Matt's advances. Despite all of Matt's pleading, even a proposal of marriage; Christine just wouldn't succumb to the pressure. Christine and Matt moved on to college and eventually marriage to others, but, despite the fact that she always rebuffed Matt's sexual advances, Christine always wondered what a sexual experience with Matt would have been like.

The notice in the paper cemented her resolve to explore all of her options.

She called him and they had lunch, then dinner, and finally sex. The relationship lasted three years and finally Matt decided that he wanted marriage with Christine and, this time, he wasn't taking no for an answer.

Matt truly was Christine's soul mate. She knew that her marriage to Kevin was a status quo marriage and that she was protecting her children's future and their well-being by trying to make the marriage work. She knew that Kevin would be unfaithful again, and that she doubted she would be able to endure another episode of "patching things up." Christine could not allow herself to be torn apart by tradition and customs again. She could not ignore the voice in her heart pleading with her to permit Matt to be part of her life. Christine knew that Matt would be an excellent and competent father for her children and would accept them into his family with open arms.

However, Christine chose to remain in her marriage and Matt resolved himself to wait for her until her children were out of high school.

Why? Matt would never be able to provide the type of lifestyle for her children that Kevin could, and she did not want to rely on Matt to furnish any financial support. Matt would also have to support his child. She knew that Kevin would not support the children if she divorced him. Christine did not want her children to be subjected to "step" siblings or "step" parents, and the thought of her working while her children were young was out of the question.

Christine's rationale was that she and her children would have to suffer the consequences during a very important time in their lives, time that would go by all too quickly. Her children would never have the opportunity to grow up in the kind of atmosphere that Christine believed would most benefit them if she chose Matt.

She would not compromise these values, just as she would not compromise her virginity before marriage.

This was the best thing to do for Christine according to her beliefs and circumstances. Christine believed that her children would suffer consequences if she separated them from their father through divorce. Whether she was aware that her children could intuitively be conscious that something was going on with mommy and daddy was a different story. Christine's daily demeanor was intense and sullen and it was evident that she suffered outwardly from this dilemma. But she honestly believed that her self-fulfillment must be sacrificed for the greater good of her children. She took an honest assessment of the good and bad consequences of her situation and potential actions and decided that she would have more pain than pleasure if she divorced her husband and married Matt. Additionally, Christine is like countless women who have decided to marry, leave their chosen professions, stay at home with their children and suddenly realize that they are left in a relationship with their husbands that is empty. They realize that they do not have the resources or the wherewithal to protect themselves or their children if they chose to go out into the world and attain any autonomy. They do not have the self-confidence or the energy to make a move out on their own because they are frightened of what society will demand from them.

Or, on the other side of the coin, was Christine following the morally righteous path? Was her decision based on what society expected her to do or was it the best possible decision for her circumstances? What choice would she have made if Matt had been financially "better off" than Kevin was? Would it have been a factor?

Debra decided at the age of twenty to explore sex and her sexuality in every aspect. Her goal was to sleep with as many men as she felt comfortable with. She needed to explore her sexuality by experience in order to know how sexually competent she was. She sowed her "wild oats."

She experimented with every sexual scenario and in a period of six years came to the conclusion that she wanted stability and monogamy. She decided that marriage was her way of settling down. After two years of marriage she found that she was not sexually fulfilled.

Her husband met her every expectation but he could not continue to satisfy her sexual needs. Additionally, he needed her to respond "correctly" to him sexually to meet his needs. He wanted her to moan during sex and wear certain clothing and shoes.

Debra realized that in the game of life you cannot give what you do not have and you cannot receive what you already have. Debra did not need a man to prove anything about her or who she was. She did not need a man to tell her she was sexy, because she already knew she was. She was secure in herself.

Society sometimes idealizes marriage as a pinnacle of human existence, but many people, like Debra, realize that some goals cannot be realistic. People and society have high expectations regarding marriage, but these expectations do not always necessarily fulfill people's personal expectations. The ideal that is espoused by society is one person for all of the life of the marriage, until death do you part and many people cannot realistically reach this goal.

More often than not, married couples find that their spouse does not fulfill their own expectations, but they settle for them because they appease the social institution of marriage that brings children and other gratifying life experiences.

Some people, therefore, elect to have affairs and remain in their marriage. They maintain that choosing an affair doesn't imply undermining marriage but meets their own personal needs. The fact of the matter is that they want and need to explore their own needs but they will not run away from their marriage.

Affairs are usually a cheating game and become destructive to marriage. However, many find this a more acceptable alternative than abandoning the security they depend on at home. This is the reason that adultery is such a prevalent factor. Many people continue to have affairs and still remain married. They believe that affairs are personal and private, and do not have to inform their spouses or become public. The reality is that many adults have contemplated affairs without necessarily abandoning what marriage brings into their lives.

IN THE FINAL ANALYSIS

Let us imagine that the life that you are comfortable with and know intimately suddenly begins fraying at the seams because you are involved in an extra-marital affair. All the time and effort that you have invested in your marriage becomes lost. Failure and humiliation loom around you because life as you have known it is being destroyed.

You must decide the circumstances. The goals and aspirations and expectations that you once held to are gone. This experience can be both liberating and devastating. You may think that you will have a fresh start, but you must realize that there will be a new set of problems. More importantly, you will still be faced with yourself and all of your shortcomings. You will need a great deal of energy and self-confidence to follow through with any decision you may chose.

Affairs can be a painful, life-changing experience. Unfortunately, there are no right or wrong answers to questions about what is the right thing for you to do for your particular situation. We are all governed by our culture, religion and social upbringing. Of the many, many women who find themselves grappling with an affair, all experience unique circumstances.

The statistics are overwhelming. Some surveys say eighty-five percent of all married people have had extramarital affairs, some say sixty percent. Most people are governed by the cultural and societal status quo and try to do the right thing. However, no one really knows exactly what the right thing is for him or her to do.

All of the reasons given by experts and all of the consequences that can afflict your emotional, physical and financial well-being are staggering, but still the statistics stare us in the face.

CHAPTER FIVE

Choices

"*Choice is the rudder that guides each person's destiny.*"
Peter Megargee Brown

"*The first act of freedom is to choose it.*"
William James

WEIGHING YOUR CHOICES FOR YOUR FUTURE

You are the person who helps avoid friction and chaos within your family. However, when you are involved in an extra-marital affair, you are opening yourself, your time, your body, and your mind to another person. You will be spreading your energies very thin, and this will eventually take its toll on you, the "glue" that holds the family together.

Generally, if you are not preoccupied with your new relationship, you are a major force in your family that prevents internal conflict and enables everything to flow smoothly in your household. Think of all that you accomplish in any given day specifically for your family. Think of how much you enable your family to accomplish all that they can. Most of your day involves nurturing and caring for the family, and if you work outside the home or volunteer, taking a lover, will mean an increased drain of your resources.

Obviously, you are not content in your life and are seeking fulfillment for yourself, but you must realize that you will have negative consequences to pay. Since you are the person who is responsible for your family's progress and improvement, you may be extremely agitated about the effects of your decisions upon your most treasured possession, your children. As a result, your health may be compromised as well as your contentment and you could eventually lose your self-respect.

Let's back up a few paces. These statements are not meant to be taken in a derogatory light or to mean that an extra-marital affair is wrong or right. To condemn or condone an extra-marital affair is wrong because the individual circumstances must always be taken into account. The purpose here is to make certain that women do not become victims of their choices. This is not a judgment.

In this situation, you will be compromising all that is familiar to you and what you have grown to be accustomed to. Are you ready to handle more people making demands and having expectations from you while sapping more of your energy?

When you are involved in an extra-marital affair, responsibility weighs heavily in your everyday life. You have assumed the responsibility of wife, mother, friend and lover. You have always worn many hats. Everyone relies on you to carry on your end of being a devotedly attached and nurturing person. It will be difficult, to say the least, to add another layer to your mantle or, even worse, to detach yourself from the roots that you have so very carefully cultivated.

Suddenly your world is at an impasse. Life is more complicated than ever. Everything that made sense is now senseless.

It's hard to say what is wrong or right or moral. Everything is never in black and white. Making a decision would be easy if we had absolutes, but unfortunately we all know that life gives us new challenges every day. If we could look into the future and realize the consequences of our actions, and see the results, there would be no agonizing choices. This doesn't happen.

But when we plan and weigh all of the pros and cons, we can find the courage to accept and deal with our consequences. Surviving because of the courage of our convictions can be gratifying and rewarding because we will have accepted our choice with the realization that there will be adjusting and readjusting. We will be affirming our existence, building our character and expressing our creativity.

There is a caution here however; we must keep in mind that our choices often come at a heavy cost to others.

RESPONSIBILITY

You've heard this word responsibility time and time again, and somehow you just can't seem to ever imagine that you wouldn't accept responsibility for a choice you make. You have never imagined that you would not hold yourself accountable for your actions or would not be capable of rational conduct. As a wife, mother and friend, you consider yourself reliable, trustworthy and credible.

You hold your actions in the highest esteem because you respect life and all that it has to offer. Mention the word responsibility and you envision that you are the epitome of the word.

What happened? How did you allow all of your life aspirations to be traded-off for a lustful whim?

Or was it? Your affair is not something that you have taken lightly. First of all, you have been extremely careful to guard your family from the truth and protect yourself from being caught. Since you are so responsible, you have made sure that you have covered all of your tracks. The thought of ever being "found out" is the furthest thing from your mind. You're responsible! It's like believing that when you grow up you will be grown up.

When your marriage has deteriorated to the point where you have engaged in an extra-marital affair, you eventually realize that you must decide to either stay in the marriage or terminate it. With your indiscretion you have violated the trust, confidence and love of your spouse. While some may believe an act that causes this result is immoral behavior, and others believe it is neutral, the fact remains that you have taken a step toward dissolving your family and causing the suffering of your husband and children. Acting in a responsible manner and making a conscious choice to divorce or work to strengthen the marriage is the best solution.

Tolerance and reasonableness by your spouse can only go so far. You have to decide if you are serious about your marriage vows and the marriage itself. When you continue the affair in secret, you are compromising the dignity and respect you have for your spouse. Choose to be responsible and decide to stop living a hellish existence at your own expense.

When you decide to marry someone, you make the decision to commit to him and remain by his side no matter what the road ahead carries with it. But if you cultivate a more enriching life without your spouse you have no choice but to admit that things are not working out, or continue your deceit until, in all likelihood, you are discovered. Then the choice may be taken out of your hands.

SAVING YOUR MARRIAGE

If you decide to try to save your marriage and make it work you must begin by regrouping and regaining your initial and mutual ambitions and goals that brought you together to marriage in the first place. Mutual values that both of you upheld and mutual achievements and expectations such as children, career goals, or academic challenges that you shared. A value is anything that gives and directs an individual's purpose and meaning of life such as enhancement of each other's dreams by being available for each other emotionally, socially or financially. This value could be embodied in a person, a belief or an institution. When the value is in a person then that person is of ultimate significance. A belief enhances the purpose of living; for example, if you believe that motherhood helps to build society then you will put every effort into becoming a good parent. We interpret reality according to our beliefs and how we prefer to invest our resources in order to articulate our beliefs. Institutions embody values such as marriage

Perhaps you feel that by telling your husband that you had an extra-marital affair you can make your marriage stronger. Many husbands can never get over the fact that they have been betrayed and this could loom very large as a source of major discontent in your marriage. If you decide to tell your husband and he is unable to reconcile and be satisfied to let it go this discontent will erode your marriage. Many people think that over time they will heal, but just as many people dispute this because they cannot erase the hurt from their hearts that always lingers.

Barry L. Duncan, Psy.D and Joseph W. Rock, Psy.D, in their book *Overcoming Relationship Impasses: Ways to Initiate Change When Your Partner Won't Help*, offer some valuable insights. They say that "surviving an affair in a marriage is like surviving the death of a loved one, because the married relationship as it was prior to the discovery of the affair is forever lost." It is difficult to get over the hurt of the loss of a loved one but you eventually begin to accept the loss and realize that you will always hurt to some degree. Your husband will have to accept the fact that the relationship as it was before is dead and he will need to experience and express the entire range of emotions associated with the affair such as hurt, anger and betrayal.

While your husband is going through this grieving process he will need to discuss his feelings openly and honestly. However, you will try to cope with the situation by trying to diminish the reality of its occurrence and with-draw from talking about it ever happening. You will want to ignore this ugly episode in your life and your husband will want to talk about his hurt. The result will be that you will feel constantly under attack and your husband will feel misunderstood because he is trying to work out his frustrations with your betrayal. The foundation of your marriage will be on shaky grounds.

Let's examine a common situation between Phyllis and Larry similar to Duncan and Rock's example used in their book, which is an illustration of possible consequences you can face if you elect to disclose your infidelity to your hus-band. They had been married for about twelve years. Over time, a lack of intimacy and restlessness developed in their relationship. Phyllis began an affair with a man with whom she worked. The man confessed the affair to his wife and told her he wanted a divorce. The man's wife confronted Phyllis and then she called Larry and told him all of the details of the affair.

Phyllis and Larry decided to seek professional help to save their marriage. They were able to work through a lot of the hurt, anger and guilt. Their marriage seemed to be working. Until Phyllis's job forced her to go out of town to attend a convention. When she returned, Larry began a crossfire examination of the chain of events at the conven-tion. He wanted to know every detail of what she experi-enced and where and with whom she was with at the con-vention. Phyllis honestly and sensitively answered every question. However, Larry could not withdraw and more and more questions and suspicions developed. Larry be-gan to exclude Phyllis from his day to day life, they never had sex and they hardly ever talked. Ultimately, Phyllis became furious and confronted Larry for his criticism and insinuations. Phyllis protected her integrity and told Larry that she had been giving him no reason to mistrust her. Larry told her that he could never forgive her for her indiscretion and that he could never trust her again. He refused to go back to therapy and he did not want a divorce. Phyllis could not make the re-commitment and forced Larry to divorce her.

Professional therapists, including Duncan and Rock, suggest that Phyllis continue to allow Larry to work out all of his anxiety and talk and question constantly. Phyllis must encourage Larry to express all of his feelings about the affair to her and she must listen and she cannot become defensive. She must allow Larry the opportunity to grieve by investigating every possible aspect of the affair until he can understand and accept her affair.

Let's examine the idea of not telling your spouse that you had an affair and how you will cope. Keeping the affair secret is advisable when telling would be so hurtful to the spouse that more would be lost than gained. Many women are fiercely determined to sustain their marriages and protect their children as well as their lovers and their lover's families and find it pointless and inane to disclose their infidelity to their husbands. This point must not be taken lightly. There are many women who have engaged in extra-marital affairs who realize that the price they would pay from society is far worse than the anxiety and guilt that they may have holding the affair in their hearts forever. In fact, many women believe that the affair was liberating and enlightened them to fulfill their potential by finding satisfaction for this lust to better themselves in other ways than extra-marital relationships such as going to school or embarking on a career. The fact is that the extra-marital affair was instrumental to their realizing that they were not satisfied with their lives and the affair encouraged them to grow in ways that they never expected. They were unfulfilled in their marriages and they moved on to solve the problem with the affair, which led them to understand that they needed the emotional nourishment that the affair provided. Therefore, the affair helped them grow personally.

As a result, the affair rescued their marriages and filled the emptiness in them until they realized what was more important in their lives, their families. Their loyalty to their husbands and their desire to protect their children outweigh their personal needs and disclosing their secret would be more harmful than good.

Despite the fact that many women today are freer and involved in more autonomous democratic marriages they still bear the brunt of the work load at home and are still being overpowered in private by men who influence them in one way or another. The dichotomy of the matter is that women have found that they must be unfaithful to their husbands in order not to deceive themselves.

If you decide to reconcile yourself to nurture your marriage back to health, whether you disclose your infidelity or not, you will be forced to make many difficult decisions as well as commit to a great deal of hard work and dedication. Will you be up to working on a marriage that you were so dissatisfied with that you decided to seek fulfillment from another person?

The decision to rekindle your marriage will mean that you must make an effort to have a meaningful closeness that you haven't had in a long while with your spouse. You must be willing to make yourself vulnerable again to your spouse and, more importantly, your spouse will have to allow himself to be vulnerable. You will find it necessary to establish interdependency and hold each other accountable again with obligations toward creating a sound relationship. Your relationship will again become very important. In effect, you will have to decide to limit your freedom, which is what marriage must do to promote a strong bond of trust between a husband and wife.

The modern marriage promise assumes that a couple's relationship will be built on mutual trust. Trust enables each partner to affirm his or her own security and the rewards of the marriage bond. Partners bring their own personalities into marriage, along with their attitudes, values and feeling. In the case of an attempt to repair a marriage, each partner's personality will determine if the intimacy that both once shared can be retrieved or redeveloped.

Without mutual trust it is difficult to maintain a meaningful marriage. An extra-marital affair betrays the trust your partner had in you. When you betrayed your partner's trust, you betrayed a basic confidence and faith that your partner had in your relationship, that is, he expected that you would not hurt him.

Extra-marital affairs undermine the foundation of trust your partner had to develop to be able to keep his promise to be faithful to the marriage vows. Marriage assumes an emotional investment built on trust. Psychologists overwhelmingly believe that the ability to trust is absolutely necessary for intimacy.

Getting back the intimacy you once enjoyed in your relationship will be a challenge, but if both you and your spouse are committed to shared goals it can be achieved. Both of you will have to decide if you are willing to take the risk that you will be able to understand truly how each feels in any given important situation. You will be re-committing yourselves to be emotionally close again and permit the relationship to grow without feeling smothered or restricted. Perhaps you will be able to draw on your past foundation of positive mutual experiences to rebuild the bond you once had together.

SEEKING HELP

Ending your marriage is not merely an event in your life; it is a process that has many sides. Emotions, behaviors and thoughts are all involved. Ending a marriage usually occurs after some emptiness, disorder or turbulence has been in existence in the relationship for some time. Most marriages that end in divorce do so after the marriage has been going badly for at least months but often years. Usually it takes more than a year to deliberate and make a final decision.

If you have reason to believe that you can work everything out with your spouse and you are willing to make some compromises, maybe it would be worth your while to seek professional help to see if the marriage can be saved. Professional counseling can help you decide where you want your relationship to go.

Marriage counseling may help you rekindle the love that once existed; however, this accomplishment takes a lot of hard work and dedication. Additionally, it means that you have again committed yourself to your marriage.

Counseling may help you understand what you expect from your spouse and what your spouse expects from you. It may help you to outline the different phases of your relationship. For example, perhaps you have certain ideals about your spouse that are unrealistic. You believe that romantically your spouse should fulfill a certain fantasy, and when this does not happen, you become disillusioned. Maybe you had an imaginary perception of what romance should be and your spouse didn't meet that expectation. Your counselor will help you sort out the different phases you have been experiencing and help you decide what the best course of action for you will be.

When you were first married you and your spouse had goals, and you expected to have rewards for attaining those goals together. What you envisioned was a house, money in the bank, satisfying jobs, etc. But along the way you realized that your union isn't as strong and secure as you would have liked it to be. Suddenly the material items don't seem so important.

Over time you feel that something is missing. Things are not working the way you planned, so you try to love your spouse harder, to give more, or to be sexier. Perhaps you can do this by dressing more provocatively or wearing trendier clothing or even wearing sexy nightgowns.

Perhaps you believe that you should accept that this is the way marriages are supposed to be; you find it necessary to be more realistic. You tone down your expectations or go a different path and seek fulfillment through an extra-marital affair. Your affair will supply you with the high-quality emotional and physical closeness that your marriage lacks. You hope that this will bring you personal happiness. However, an affair can be a desperate attempt to re-create the romance of your early married years, but of course an affair does not have the same kind of stresses as a marriage, so it is not a fair comparison. Instead you find yourself with a strong feeling of loneliness and lack of closeness. When you discuss these feelings with your spouse, they always go unanswered and you feel even more distant and isolated.

Emotional bruises and torments that you have suppressed—feeling rejected, not being needed, or appreciated, or not being important in your spouse's life, seem to mount. Maybe you have been more tearful and irritable more often. Negative emotions begin to multiply and you become even more uncertain. You begin to doubt if you can ever really love your spouse again. You then begin to withdraw from him or lash out, expecting him to help you both reach a compromise.

Sexual drive becomes practically non-existent. You either refuse to have sex with your partner or have sex only as a duty. Maybe you use sex to lessen the feeling of being deprived of closeness, or you have sex in a desperate attempt to try to hold on to your marriage. You reach out to personal friends or family about your relationship that is failing and you aren't even sure exactly what you want.

At this point your counselor can help you find out if you have any feeling left at all for your partner, either positive or negative. You become passive and insensitive because there is no longer any opposition in your relationship. You feel you don't want to hurt anyone, but at the same time you don't look forward to spending any time with your husband. You don't miss him when he goes away, you don't want to go home when he is around, and you don't look forward to his homecoming.

Through therapy maybe you have found that you no longer love your spouse. You still have to make a decision to get out of the relationship—a separation or divorce—or to remain in the marriage. You may decide that even though you no longer have the emotional closeness you once had, you will remain married because you are at a stage in life where you believe there would be no chance for another positive relationship. You decide not to leave your spouse because of your religious convictions or because of guilt, pity or your poor health. You decide that you would never be able to leave your spouse because of your financial position, or that you would never be able to cope with the fact that your marriage has failed. Perhaps you understand all of the hardships that divorce causes for children and decide that you will cope before you subject them to any pain.

Both of you will have to reaffirm your needs, desires and expectations, and re-commit to what you want from each other. You will have to admit that you have been angry. You will have to acknowledge that you depend on your spouse. You will have to acknowledge the fact that you will have to make compromises. You will have to acknowledge the fact that you and your spouse are dedicated to the success of your relationship and no longer will think about alternatives that would harm the security of the relationship. You will have to prove your commitment over and over again to your spouse and be willing to work through conflicts that will inevitably arise. You and your spouse will have to agree to difficult soul-searching in order for this effort to be successful. In effect you will have to re-attach yourselves to each other and rekindle your previous attachment toward each other.

COPING WITH THE EFFECTS OF DIVORCE

You have decided that you want to divorce your spouse. You will experience much turbulence for unspecified periods of time since no one really knows how long it will take for anyone to come to grips with the reality of divorce. It may depend on how long it takes you to adjust to new situations or how long you were married. How much time you had to prepare for your marriage to break up will determine how well you will adjust. Factors such as your economic situation, new love relationships, your support network of friends, and the quality of the relationship you have with your spouse all must be taken into consideration for you to be at ease with the divorce process.

Perhaps you were lonely before you divorced but now you feel even more isolated. You may find it difficult to cope with your loneliness. This could be caused by the fact that you may have to readjust your social life. Keep this in mind before you divorce and make sure that your network of friends will clearly support you and spend time with you when you are facing the lonely days.

Typically our society promotes couples. You might begin to feel frustration to live up to the social norms of couples at various social functions, such as dinner, family parties or charity events with spouses, if you are expected. Traditionally, your married friends tend to desert you, especially if they were mutual friends of you and your husband. Dating, if your affair is over, will be a new and different experience for you and may help you fit into your single friend's social lives more readily. Keep in mind that you may have to initiate a date. You may feel a lack of self-confidence with this idea but keep trying. Ask your friends for help, if needed, to get off the mark.

You will have to have a considerable amount of patience with yourself to carefully cultivate a meaningful relationship and it may take a few years. The superficiality of the social scene may grate on you for some time. Longing for a continuous close relationship may make you lonelier, but in time you can find a new partner who will help to satisfy your needs.

During and after a divorce you may be maintaining two households for a period of time, and this will result in some economic hardships. You will have to change your lifestyle and make additional sacrifices; for example, it might be very hard for a divorced woman to establish credit. Except for totally self-sufficient women, the lowered standard of living following a divorce puts enormous pressure on a woman's self-esteem and general competence. This pressure may eventually help her grow her self-esteem and competence to considerable heights, but there is almost always a difficult period of self-searching she must go through. Hardships can and do befall divorced women.

If you have children and you are granted custody, you will have expenses that you must consider in the divorce agreement. The ultimate financial burden of the children may fall on your shoulders, and you must be prepared for all expenses and then some. Make sure that your settlement award is sufficient to cover the fact that you may have lower earnings than your husband because of additional expenses for the children. Make sure that you have an effective means of collecting your support and securing it so you will not have the added burden of fighting for it in court. Finding a competent attorney to help you through the process of divorce should be of paramount importance to you because an attorney is essential to guide you toward your goals of autonomy and financial freedom.

If you were in a marriage that lacked fun and emotional closeness and included few common interests, you may find that divorce is a positive step for you. You are no longer subjected to the rigors of living in a bad marriage and you may find yourself better off emotionally. If you willingly accept the challenge to use your skills and resources to survive and manage your affairs successfully, you will be able to take control of your life. This control will improve your self-esteem and give you greater competence in all aspects of your life.

If you believe that you have acted responsibly throughout the entire process of the divorce and managed the stress, your choices will probably have a positive impact on your emotional well-being because you have taken charge of your own destiny.

CHILDREN

This is not the case for children, however, and it is wise to understand going into a divorce just how difficult that change will be for your children. Depending on their age, they will experience powerful negative emotions such as fear, anger and guilt, and will require a considerable amount of time, attention and affection to reassure them that they will not be neglected. The powerful sense of loss that they will be subjected to, as well as their own lack of power to prevent the inevitable, will be very stressful for them. This will take its toll on you, and you will have to be aware of how they are thinking and reacting to the situation to understand fully the impact of divorce to their world.

Life as your children have known it will be seriously disrupted. Children under three simply won't understand, but will need to be given information as they get older. Children three to six will be bewildered and angry. Children seven to ten will be bewildered, angry, sad and perhaps feel guilty and torn between their parents. Children eleven through sixteen or seventeen will be the most disrupted because they have the most established routines. It will take great effort to prevent them from acting out their negative feelings through violence, drugs, alcohol, sex and so on. Grades will probably also be affected.

Children may experience a new school, moving, child-care and even stepsisters and brothers. Your care and understanding will be needed more than ever, especially in the beginning when everyone is adjusting. Remember their ideal is for you and your husband to remain together no matter what the circumstances. If they are feeling guilty or believe they have caused the divorce, assure them that this is not the case. Also assure them that you and your ex-husband still love them.

Children will experience a confusing jumble of emotions. They may believe that you and your spouse will abandon them, and they will probably seek constant reassurance to become secure in their new environment. If they feel responsible for your break-up, they may believe that they can reunite you and your spouse. If you or your spouse are still emotionally attached or hesitating on certain issues, this will fuel the children's desire to hope that you will reconcile. If there is no hope of reconciliation, be sure to let your children know this in a firm but loving way.

Children can become angry and take that anger out on you. They may blame you or your spouse for disrupting their lives. Your children may become depressed and require psychological counseling. They may feel as if someone close to them has died, and they will be right: their family unit is no more.

The divorce of parents is very traumatic for children and it must be considered very carefully before you divorce to give them time to adjust to the shock. It is usually beneficial for both you and your spouse to break the news to them together and reassure them that both of you will be available for them. It is also important to give them specific reasons for the divorce in terms they can understand so they won't believe it is their fault. Avoid being critical of each other or degrading each other in front of your children. Whatever happened, they still love both of you.

Tell them exactly what they can expect in the future. Make them aware of the fact that there will be some confusion for a while, but that you will be available to help them adjust. Professional counseling for the children as well as family therapy will help in many situations.

STEP-FAMILIES

While these are the most obvious repercussions of divorce on your children, you will still have to consider stepfamilies and their challenges if you ever decide to remarry. The rules for stepparents and stepchildren have never been clearly defined and are always a source of confusion to the new family as well as outsiders. Realize that there may always be competition and jealousy among you, your new spouse, and your children and stepchildren. These feelings can cause unpleasant intensity and become another source of potential conflict. You will also have to establish how you will interact with your former in-laws and your own family.

Divorce will bring many challenges and heart-wrenching days, so try to visualize your role in overcoming all the above-mentioned obstacles to make your life more rewarding, enjoyable and stable.

Samantha and Edgar's story is an example of a woman who carefully weighed all of the consequences of divorce and made her decision accordingly. Samantha and Edgar, in their mid-forties, had been married for twenty-four years. On the outside, their marriage seemed to be solid. They had one seventeen-year old son who was going off to college in about one year. Their families shared a deep bond and extended history. It was customary to have Edgar's parents spend weekends with Samantha and Edgar, and every other Sunday Samantha and Edgar would eat at Samantha's mom's home with her entire family. Their families were always accessible for babysitting so Samantha never had to hire a baby-sitter. Their families frequently went on vacation together and Edgar hired his brother and Samantha's sister and brother-in-law to work for him.

Despite all this togetherness, Samantha's father and brother both had many extra-marital affairs. Samantha never had strong convictions for or against infidelity. She believed her father when he told her that sometimes circumstances warranted him to seek affection from someone other than his wife. Her parent's marriage was an arranged marriage where their immigrant parents (Samantha's grandparents) chose Samantha's father and mother to continue the prosperous family histories. Although her mother suffered the torment of her father's many infidelities; Samantha never understood her mother's agony because Samantha and her mother never understood each other. She had no empathy for her mother, and the two of them fought constantly. Her mother was always taking her frustrations out on Samantha and her siblings.

Edgar came from a home where family values and commitment were the cornerstone of life. His mother and father were devoted to each other, and Edgar and his brother were the center of their loving attention.

Edgar rescued Samantha from her unhappy family life when she was twenty. He was a year older. They had a fairytale wedding with all of the trimmings. Edgar and Samantha had mutual goals and aspirations and worked together planning careers, building their first home at a very young age and carefully planning their family. Samantha was always available for Edgar and she supported Edgar's drive to succeed. He often said, "Samantha inspired him to achieve all of his goals."

Samantha stayed home, took care of their son and entertained Edgar's business associates. Edgar was a driven man and obsessive about achieving success at all costs. Their life revolved around material gain and his career goals.

Samantha met Richard at the mall. He sold her all of Edgar's expensive custom-tailored suits. One day they had lunch and the next week dinner. The next week they were meeting at the local Holiday Inn.

Samantha was very isolated and lonely because Edgar was always preoccupied with his business. Their life centered on "the business." Edgar exhausted himself mentally, physically and emotionally at work during the day and most evenings. Samantha tried to keep herself involved with business issues and help Edgar, but she suddenly realized that their life was never going to be without chaos and trauma caused by day to day operations of running a business. That's just the way it is when you have your own business. She had to get off the merry-go-round. The final straw came when Edgar took her away for their twentieth wedding anniversary and brought along his cell phone. He talked to his associates on the phone through all their "intimate" meals and even when they were in bed. The cell phone bill for the trip was almost one thousand dollars.

When the business started to show some profit Edgar changed. He would subtly mention how hard he worked and sacrificed and that he was the reason for the family's being able to realize all of the material gain that they enjoyed. He constantly reminded Samantha that she did not contribute to the success of the business. Samantha felt that she was very much a part of the business success because she, too, sacrificed a great deal. Samantha realized that the only relationship she had with Edgar was a business one and her worth to him was only as far as the business progressed. And to make matters worse, sex with Edgar was a one-way street, after working from five A.M. until seven P.M. then coming home and taking endless phone calls, Edgar was exhausted and he was never available for Samantha.

Richard talked to Samantha. He noticed what she was wearing and complimented her. He listened intently to her every word and he shared his innermost thoughts with her. During their long discussions together they discovered that they had a great deal in common. Making love with Richard was the most gratifying sexual experience that Samantha had ever had. Richard knew exactly how to make love to a woman. Edgar and Samantha were both virgins when they married.

Samantha and Richard kept the affair going for almost six years. Because Richard was not married and had no children, he was very tolerant of Samantha and her time and never made unreasonable demands for her attention. He understood how torn she was and that, even though she admitted that she never really loved Edgar, he was willing to give her as much time as she needed to decide if the two of them should be married.

Samantha decided that she needed freedom without any strings attached. She wanted more than material things and longed for intimacy, support, friendship and mutually satisfying sex that Edgar never gave her. She never dated extensively and she didn't know what it was like to do so. She decided she would leave Edgar. She became a paralegal, got a job and started saving money for her own future. She waited until after her son graduated from high school, before she broke the news to Edgar that she wanted the divorce.

Samantha continued to see Richard. Their relationship became more satisfying to her because she didn't have to spread herself between her husband, son and Richard. They were able to truly bond and their relationship matured beyond both of their expectations. Two years after Samantha's divorce was final, she and Richard married.

Samantha and Edgar's marriage is an example of marrying to fulfill social or stereotypical mandates. Samantha believed that Edgar would take her from her family and rescue her to a better life. It is an example of one of the reasons why there is a strong need to better prepare our daughters about what the institution of marriage demands for women and how they will need to cope and be successful and happy within the institution. It is an example of the customs and cultures regarding marriage in the past and how these customs and cultures still reflect the mindset today. Edgar never questioned his role in marriage, to bring families together and have children, and his role to provide for them. This was the example that his family perpetuated and expected of him and Edgar was satisfied fulfilling this role. However, Samantha was not satisfied and her dissatisfaction became evident when she found something lacking enough to pursue an extra-marital affair. Perhaps her idea of a better life with Edgar would have been more realistic had Samantha realized all of the demands and expectations that the institution of marriage has on women. Yes, Samantha appears to be self-centered, but she realized that the goals and aspirations she had devoted herself to all of her married life were Edgar's idea of what life and marriage and success were all about. Samantha wanted more depth in her life and an understanding, loving partner. She wanted to work at her own career other than Edgar's business because a pursuit of her own would be more satisfying. Samantha would have been better informed had she and Edgar discussed each other's expectations. Although they had shared goals and aspirations for children, business and material gain Samantha wanted more of a meaningful close relationship. Perhaps she should have understood this better before she married and perhaps she should have known the kind of life she imagined in marriage before marriage. Because Samantha was able to understand finally what she wanted for herself she was able to make the transition with Richard smoother and more acceptable to herself and her son. Her son was an adult when she made the announcement to divorce and he was not living at home. He was in college and actively involved in his own life's aspirations. Her son's dependency on Samantha was considerably less than when he was younger. Although it took patience and timing on her part, to be considerate of everyone involved, she was able to realize her dreams. Yes, it may have been a fairy-tale ending but because of her patience, planning and consideration Samantha made the transition much smoother and more acceptable.

CHAPTER SIX

*No Sex...
No Affair?*

"Sex is the biggest nothing of all time."
Andy Warhol

*"What I like about masturbation is that you don't
have to talk afterwards."*
Milos Forman

"Enjoy yourself. If you can't enjoy yourself, enjoy somebody else."
Jack Schaefer

DEFINITION OF THE TERM "AFFAIR"

From the book *Sexual Arrangements: Marriage and the Temptation of Infidelity* by Janet Reibstein, Ph.D. and Martin Richards, Ph.D.:

> "The term affair describes a sexual relationship between people who are not married to each other but at least one of the partners in the relationship is married to someone else. Other terminology has been used to signify the same phenomenon, including infidelity and adultery. Both of these terms carry a moral judgement: adultery alludes to the biblical injunction against it; infidelity means unfaithful, since an infidel is one who breaks faith and a moral commitment."

"The word affair does not carry these moralistic overtones, but it does perhaps imply something frivolous. The difficulty of finding the appropriate terminology is related to both the difficult feelings aroused by the phenomenon and the variations in the phenomenon itself. Some affairs are frivolous, unimportant in the larger scheme of the participants' lives, and sometimes short-lived. Others are serious, sometimes even life-changing, and sometimes virtually life-long. Some are like parallel marriages, others intermittently important, others almost forgotten."

Reibstein and Richards further state that "affairs implicitly pose a challenge to our prevailing beliefs about marriage. As such, they shake our complacency. For a moment we have to think, 'Could this be me?' or 'Why not me?' They further challenge our ideas about marriage being a partnership in which we own or possess our spouse, an implicit code by which most marriages live: 'My wife/my husband.' Clearly, if a spouse can go to bed with someone else, the other partner does not possess that spouse."

Reibstein and Richards contend that "this possessiveness is particularly true for husbands, since Western marriage grew out of patriarchy in which families, including wives, belonged to husbands. And the still-strong double standard growing out of that patriarchy makes having affairs a greater transgression for women than for men. Affairs also contradict the very vows that are supposed to bind most marriages: thou shalt forsake all others, in sickness and in health, till death us do part." Remember marriage is a contract, and we don't expect ourselves to default on other contracts.

Let's explore some of the components of an affair and some of the experiences that you will encounter when you begin an affair.

ESCAPING REALITY

Have you ever met someone that excites you intellectually? Your mind seems to come alive when you talk to him. You seem to remember every scholarly opinion and geographic boundary whenever your eyes meet. The connection you share is on an indisputably higher plane than with anyone else you have encountered. Your mind is challenged to discuss any topic that is laid out on the table. When something stimulating crosses your mind, you immediately think of this person and long for his opinion. Usually this person is a professional colleague, and opportunities always present themselves for the two of you to spend long time periods together.

Even though this person is stimulating to you in many respects, sexual tension does not exist and the desire for intimacy through sex in not a factor in the relationship. You gain a tremendous amount of satisfaction simply through intellectual interaction and do not feel compelled to explore the relationship any further. The issue is that you are desired in a way other than sexually, and your desire is stimulating senses other than sexual senses.

Extra-marital relationships that do not involve sex are a form of escape. Seeking fulfillment through intellectual stimulation or enabling ourselves to indulge in fantasies that we have never been exposed to with our spouse helps us to liberate the needs we hold secretly in our innermost selves. We all feel compelled at many points in our marriage to escape from sexual anxieties and the many frustrations of a monogamous marriage. But can we classify the intellectual attraction or the spiritual attraction or the just-for-fun attraction as an extra-marital affair? If yes, then we couldn't have stimulating friends of the opposite sex.

SPIRITUAL ATTACHMENT

Janet was a volunteer at her church. She normally spent fifteen to twenty hours a week in the rectory. Father Jim was the pastor, and Janet's work centered around tasks that he initiated with her. She enjoyed his kind, gentle and encouraging nature, and he was always very attentive and listened to her with a great deal of perception.

Their time together afforded them the opportunity to discuss many areas of present-day spirituality. Given the pastor's extensive education and experience with human suffering, his insights mesmerized Janet. They spent long hours in the rectory kitchen discussing God's grace and uncharted spiritual paths. Father Jim filled an emptiness and longing in Janet. He revealed a side of her that was hidden away. Together they opened up secrets of their humanness and deep soulful longings.

Physical contact was always a passing thought in Janet's mind, but for some reason that aspect of their relationship was implausible. Father Jim was not physically attractive to Janet. There was always occasion to brush past one another or give each other an affectionate hug or a peck on the cheek, but sexual tension just wasn't there.

The problem Janet experienced was that, when she came home from her volunteer work at church, she was emotionally exhausted. Father Jim fulfilled her spiritual hunger and that was all the attention she needed. Peter, her husband, seemed to feel that she was becoming distant in many respects from him, but he could not explain or understand just what had come over her. In his mind, Janet was obsessed with volunteer work at church and did not respond to him as she had in the past. Janet's demeanor was quiet and contemplative. This bothered Peter because he couldn't seem to interest her or arouse her. She was always on another wavelength.

Janet felt Peter's resentment build but would not attempt to ease his misgivings. She was very satisfied and refused to limit her time with Father Jim. He boosted her self-esteem and that was worth any risk on the home front. Besides, there was no sex involved.

Would this be considered an extra-marital affair? The relationship that Janet experienced with Father Jim provided an escape from the frustrations of her marriage and from sexual anxieties. The emotional commitment shared between Janet and Father Jim was not considered destructive to Janet's marriage because there was no sex involved. But what about her emotional unavailability to Peter?

Peter would never be able to come close to providing the type of stimulation that Father Jim gave to Janet, and this caused dissension in the marriage. It is difficult to understand why this would not be considered an affair to many people. And was Father Jim Janet's "lover" despite the fact that she did not go to bed with him? In this scenario most would believe that Janet was neglecting her husband. Her interest could be a sport or an animal or hobby. However, some people believe that an affair is anything that depletes your time and energy away from your spouse is considered a form of disloyalty and therefore considered to be an affair. Some people believe that it would not be considered an affair because it is simply a matter of creating distance.

EMOTIONAL STIMULATION

Marcy was a chemical engineer and her consulting position required her to travel on extensive fact-finding business trips. Her colleague, Allen, collaborated with her on many of her consults and they were very close friends.

Allen's marriage was always "on the rocks" and he would always seek Marcy's shoulder to complain about all of his troubles with his wife. Marcy was very devoted to her husband and never felt compelled to go beyond her marriage commitment. She was "satisfied."

The fact that Marcy and Allen spent a great deal of time together talking and having dinner and discussing the pitfalls of Allen's marriage didn't cause Marcy to feel that she was neglecting her husband. However, her time away from home was interfering with her marriage. She enjoyed the time spent with Allen, and when she was home she felt like something was missing. Her husband wasn't able to satisfy her need for intellectually stimulating conversation or provide a respite from the competition she felt with him to earn the most money. Allen was always available to discuss complex engineering designs and solutions as well as provide a shoulder for her to express her growing dissatisfaction with her marriage. Friendship, intellectual stimulation, no sexual tension and escape from the competitive pressure at home contributed a substantial boost to Marcy's self-esteem. She felt competent when she was with Allen. He challenged her and was able to fulfill her need to talk with someone who was on a par with her own intellect. Allen accepted and appreciated her for who she was and what she had accomplished.

Again, no sex and no sexual anxiety. Could this relationship be classified as an extra-marital affair? Was Marcy neglecting to meet the needs of her husband to fulfill her intellectual needs? Was her relationship with Allen causing dissension on her home front? Some people think that having an affair is different than using a person or interest to retreat from marital intimacy.

CYBERSEX

The millennium brings us new challenges and opportunities, and with those opportunities come the promise of more creative sexual expression. Cybersex and sexually explicit communication on the computer over the World Wide Web is fast becoming a distraction for many people. You can express your wildest fantasies and be as adventurous as your imagination will allow without ever having a face-to-face encounter. If you have the right video equipment, you can even masturbate with your "online companion" and exchange sexual pleasures all in the anonymous cocoon of your home, without contact. Some people believe that they can fulfill latent erotic passions that they would never dream of trying to express with their spouse.

People explore and express themselves more freely online than in person. Women, particularly, are much less inhibited, especially since their partner is anonymous and no one has to face anyone in the morning. Opportunities to play in a make-believe world, where they can pretend to be what they fantasize, excites many women into divulging their most intimate sexual desires and dreams.

Joyce, who recently lost her job as a legal secretary, found herself online more often that ever because she was searching for a new position. Even though she was only thirty-two, she inadvertently found herself in an "over-40-chat room." Her husband, a successful trial lawyer, wasn't interested in the benefits of computers. His staff competently took care of all of his communication needs and he didn't enjoy all of the "computer logic" necessary to manipulate the Internet or the computer. He found Joyce's passion for the "web" trivial and paid little attention to her increasing addiction.

While "chatting" one evening Joyce was invited to a private chat room by "Lion Leo." She was enticed by his intellect and quick wit. Soon they became engaged in sexually explicit conversations. After that, every moment she could steal away was spent in cyberspace with "Lion Leo." The cybersex was incredible. Joyce found herself unattracted to her husband because she could not "let herself go" as she did with "Lion Leo." Her "friend" knew her, just as she fantasized a lover would, and she began to feel "Lion Leo" understood her better than her husband understood and gave her more pleasure. He was her dream lover.

"Lion Leo" continually pushed Joyce for a phone number or secret rendezvous but Joyce resisted, believing that she was satisfied to keep him at a distance. Eventually, however, even though sex was wildly erotic, she became bored with masturbation and longed for human contact. She broke off the cyber relationship with "Lion Leo" because she intuitively felt he was truly lying Leo.

This cultural phenomenon is a growing sign of our times. It is relatively risk free, although recently, there have been cases of murders resulting from cybersex, so there is some risk. On the other hand these pseudo-affairs can blossom into real physical affairs. Additionally, you don't have to put up with unacceptable physical conditions such as smelly feet or bad breath to enjoy "good sex." It is definitely a world of make-believe created by you and there are no strings attached. The question, however, is this: When a married person and someone other than her spouse engage in "cybersex," are they having an extra-marital affair?

A SEX ONLY-AFFAIR

Let's picture a couple whose marriage is solid. They are in their mid-fifties and successful. Their children are out of the house and the wife is happily preoccupied with volunteer work, golf and making travel plans. The husband was just promoted to vice-president with his company and his responsibilities are ever increasing. He feels revitalized and has become preoccupied with his affairs at the office.

Although sex is not an all-consuming force that has dominated their marriage, their sex life has diminished to the point that it only pleases him. He comes home mentally and physically exhausted, and sex is a tension reliever for him. The wife has always been a confident and aggressive sexual partner not afraid of her sexuality. She never felt guilty about wanting and enjoying sex. After being married to her husband for thirty years, she knows and understands him very well. She feels she can tolerate this "slight drawback" because she can empathize with him and is satisfied with every other aspect of their marriage.

The only problem is that her husband is not sensitive to her needs and desires or her empathy. He is blindly ignoring her sexual needs because he feels that he gives enough to her through his dedication to his career, which is for the "good of the family," and that this lack of attention to her sexually is a temporary issue. He is assuming that she won't have the urge for sex without him.

However, this wasn't the case. The wife initiated a relationship with a trusted male friend where mutual gratification was a sex-only affair. They are both satisfied simply having sex. She believes that she is entitled to plea-surable, satisfying sex and that it is no longer just a male prerogative. She feels no guilt about admitting that she is entitled to satisfying sex and she doesn't have any remorse. The only need she has of this partner is sex.

What about this scenario? Is this considered an extra-marital affair? There is no relationship or long-term com-mitment involved, just pure, unadulterated sex. No strings attached. Just like a one-night stand that goes on until the husband recovers from his lapse of what's important in life.

Can we say that by depriving his wife of sex he drove her to a search outside of their marriage bed for the sexual satisfaction she was missing? She may have been resistant to being swept off of her feet, but she did seek temporary sex for the pure enjoyment of it. Is this a form of escape from a marriage where the husband is being very self-cen-tered? Maybe? Is this a totally immoral act designed only to emancipate her unfettered sexual desires? Or is she sim-ply meeting her needs to keep herself happy and self-ful-filled? What about her personal integrity? What conse-quences will she face because of this in the future? Will her "friend" demand a long-term relationship? Will he let go as easily as she expects?

According to Bonnie Eaker Weil, Ph.D. in her book *Adul-tery: the Forgivable Sin: Healing the Inherited Patterns of Be-trayal in Your Family*, "Webster's second definition of infi-delity includes "a breach of trust...unfaithfulness to a charge or a moral obligation." She further states "Any activity or relationship that drains too much time and energy from life with your partner is a form of unfaithfulness. That may include workaholism, obsession with children, sports or gambling addiction, as well as emotional liaisons."

CHAPTER SEVEN

Are You Ready for a Part-time Lover?

"There is no happiness; there are only moments of happiness."
Spanish Proverb

Whether you have children or you don't have children; whether you have children and you work or you are a stay at home mom, you will have the responsibility for the care of the children, the household management or both. Women do not abandon this responsibility. Very few women are not responsible. Keep this in mind if you are contemplating an extra-marital affair because your affair adds more responsibility to your plate. Your affair spreads your time a little thinner than it already is. Make no mistakes about this premise. Women innately nurture. Even if they are physically unable or emotionally unstable they struggle with this responsibility in their hearts because their family is the center of their lives. When they take a lover other than their husband they add another layer and another aspect, and more responsibility and they keep seeing the lover on a part-time basis because they do not want to take more time from their children. They become torn and their spirits become wrenched because they have that constant intrinsic desire to remain in touch with their family. It is a source of much inner turmoil. Let's look at this scenario.

LIVING THE *VIDA LOCA*

Your relationship with your lover is fun. It is warm and sensual and intense. The time spent together is affirming and accepting. Then you have to abruptly run home for family chores and responsibilities. It is almost like listening to your favorite record album and suddenly the needle scratches across the album and the joy and pleasure are rudely erased. Can you live with this?

Opportunities with your lover are stolen away from your hectic life. You are in a constant state of bewilderment because you are always torn in too many directions. You are another human being when you are with him, and you can escape the craziness of life with responsibilities that require you to wear too many hats. Your husband and children show little appreciation for all of the effort and time you invest in making their lives easier and more manageable. They maintain this attitude at the expense of your own mental health. The respite you experience when you are with your lover revitalizes and refreshes and helps you to be more tolerant of your ungrateful family. How long can you keep this up before you become mentally and physically exhausted?

You lie awake at night and sometimes pace the floors, fantasizing about what it would be like to have the freedom to share your life with your lover. The joy of waking up every day beside him and going to sleep at night with him by your side is almost too unbelievable to comprehend. Thousands of times over and over in your head you imagine getting up and picking up the phone to call him to say "goodnight." But you are so frightened that you may be caught so you resolve yourself to discontinue the torture and try to sleep. You begin to understand the importance and value of patience.

Making love, or more appropriately, having sex with your spouse feels like treachery and it disgusts you in such a way that your self-respect and self-esteem gradually decline dramatically. You are becoming a robot. It is like you have lost yourself somewhere because you cannot be who you really are. The distance between your spouse and yourself is becoming a chasm. The relationship lacks any commonality.

You don't have the courage or the vision to make the decision to end either life. You are continually vacillating between family, financial security and familiarity and what you perceive to be true self-fulfillment on the other side, with your lover. You are constantly plagued with uncertainty and not confident enough in yourself to make a choice.

When you talk to your lover, the clock is always ticking and you are constantly looking over your shoulder to make sure your children don't hear you cooing over the phone or to see if an old friend will recognize you when you and you lover finally steal a moment away out in public.

You walk around harboring your secret. It's always there and you alone are faced with the deceit. Often you never have one drop of guilt or remorse for what you are doing because it brings you so much joy and pleasure. Then you look at your children and realize the ravages of divorce and run from yourself by blotting your conduct out of your head in total disbelief knowing this is a flaw in your character but you are powerless to remedy your situation. All the while you wonder how your life ever got to this.

This is a synopsis of scenarios that are becoming all too common for women who find themselves in the predicament of living double lives by having an affair. The quiet agony that they endure is a constant reminder of their desperation. Too often they find themselves questioning their life's choices because every day they are living the consequences.

They have allowed themselves to be totally open with another person other than their spouse and they have allowed themselves to be vulnerable. They have taken great risks, and whether they like it or not, they will still have all of their feelings and still make choices.

HANGING ON

A look at the "big picture" in your life can be very revealing. Assume you have decided that something is lacking within yourself or your marriage and you have embarked on the road away from your family and your spouse. You have decided that your needs and desires, whether they are psychological or physiological, carry more weight than the needs of your family and are worth the great risk that you are taking.

You have accepted the fact that you will continue with your affair even though you must accept that your lover is not the center of your life and you are not the center of his. You can live with the idea that you can only be with your lover part-time.

Discussing this with your lover and hearing his thoughts on this predicament is always helpful. You both need to be satisfied seeing each other on a part-time basis and you both must be willing to cope with not being demanding of each other. Think about how difficult it will be to adjust your lives to fit each other in one another's lives on a part-time basis and how you will cope, not only emotionally but how you will juggle the time.

Many affairs happen without warning because couples are overcome with lust and the consequences become unnegotiated. That is, they occur without any premeditation and you are left with this inner turmoil. As a result both of you must wrestle with how to cope because you are not participating fully in each other's lives. You ask yourself how you can survive being "second fiddle" or vise versa.

CLASSIC DECEIT

The story below is classic. It is an age-old tale of love and deceit that has not changed for centuries, and it virtually tells itself. It is relevant here because it still happens, and the reasons and excuses are always the same. The married partner will not disturb the status quo and leave her spouse and family and the security of her home because the financial pressures and cultural guilt are too great.

The other partner continues to tolerate the predicament because he believes that the situation will change over time and someday she will eventually choose him. It is a fine line between a devotion to this commitment made with lovers and self-enslavement because the lovers are not free to pursue other love interests. Even though they participate fully in a full-blown love affair, they have little control of the situation and they refuse to quit the affair. It's like an addiction. How can they continue to consent to and endure the lies and sneaking around? Why do they settle for a part-time lover? What is lacking with the unmarried partner? The real question is how can they continue to sacrifice their true potential and remain in the dead-end relationship? Many allow it to go on for years.

Jennifer has been romantically involved with Rodney, her employer, for eleven years. He has been married for twenty-nine years; his relationship with Jennifer is his sixth but most enduring affair. Rodney truly loves Jennifer but he will never be able to leave his wife and three children. He tells Jennifer that his life is embedded in religious and cultural proscriptions that prohibit him from divorcing without losing his financial as well as social status. He cannot break out and make a move that would fulfill his own personal needs. Sometimes Jennifer wonders if he is simply using her to have his cake and eat it too. Jennifer settles for the first scenario.

JUSTIFICATION AND RATIONALIZATION

What's going on in the lives of these people? How do they justify or rationalize their behavior? The woman must certainly feel a loss of self-respect, where she becomes a robot to her spouse because she gives her body to him and then seeks fulfillment and pleasure with her lover. This must take a toll on self-respect. She is going through her life and existing mechanically, only going through the motions of her day to day life. Surely, she loses her honor and dignity. Adultery, lies, betrayal and loss of self-respect all have become conditions in the lives of this couple experiencing the extra-marital affair. Worst of all, they endure these hardships and still only have each other on a part-time basis.

Situations such as the ones given above cause stress. Lack of control in life and the conflict that arises when one must choose between two life-choices cause many of us to react and use defense mechanisms. We employ these defense mechanisms to help us cope and feel better about our predicament.

According to Stephen Worchel and Wayne Shebilske in their book *Psychology: Principles and Applications*, defense mechanisms are normal ways of coping with anxiety. They help us handle difficult situations. However, according to Worchel and Shebilske, because they use self-deception and distortions of reality, defense mechanisms keep us from dealing with the basic causes of stress, and thus exacerbate our problems. Worchel and Shebilske state that defense mechanisms involve finding logical reasons for behavior we might secretly regret. We seek to justify our questionable actions by providing convincing reasons, or excuses, for them. This reduces our anxiety by appearing to limit our responsibility or guilt for what is happening in our life.

Many people in an extra-marital affair persuade themselves that they are protecting their own personal sanity by escaping into an affair. They rationalize and justify their behavior by reassuring themselves that they are not harming anyone as long as they are not caught.

SPECIFIC DEFENSE MECHANISMS

Worchel and Shebilske discuss several defense mechanisms that are often used by people engaging in an extra-marital affair.

Repression involves blocking or keeping unpleasant thoughts or memories from conscious awareness. Possibly you are having an affair because you harbor hurt feelings and hostility toward your spouse, and it is difficult or impossible for you to effectively communicate these feelings and hostilities or their sources. Your affair allows you the opportunity to escape the source of your discontent. Rather than threaten or argue, you simply run for cover with someone who understands you. You never get your true feelings out in the open and on the table for debate, perhaps because you are unable to communicate with your spouse or have come to a stalemate.

Maybe you engage in suppression. Say you regularly encounter verbal abuse by your spouse, so you suppress this abuse by making a conscious effort to avoid him. For example, you escape with your lover to avoid the trauma. Although you are aware of what is going on in your marriage, your answer to it is to make a conscious effort to avoid the issues.

Displacement is an interesting defense mechanism. It involves redirecting feelings away from the individual who caused them to a safer or more available target. For example, a woman who feels torn and angry because her lover limits the time he will spend with her might act out her frustrations on her spouse and children.

When you channel the energy associated with one activity or event into a seemingly unrelated activity it is called sublimation. For example, a sex-only-and-no affection affair allows you to work the stress out of your system through sex to reduce tension and so you can more calmly proceed with your other duties. There are better ways to keep from focusing on an ugly, conflicted marriage. Counseling and therapy are definitely needed in this situation.

Another defense mechanism that Worchel and Shebilske describe is projection. All of us have qualities or feelings that we would rather not recognize or acknowledge. One way to protect ourselves from focusing on our own shortcomings is to project these shortcomings or undesirable traits on other people. Projection reduces our stress because it helps justify our actions or feelings. We think, "If other people feel that way, it's not so bad for me to feel that way." Thus, people who are filled with hostility often see people around them as being very hostile. This justifies their own actions and feelings, because it means they are reacting to other's people's hostility and are therefore not very culpable.

The reaction formation defense mechanism is the most relative to extra-marital affairs because it demonstrates how people cover up their actions and don't live up to their marriage commitment. According to Worchel and Shebilske, reaction formation is used to conceal unacceptable impulses by outwardly expressing the opposite impulse. Giving the impression of living a "normal" life and following all of the rules while engaging in a secret love affair is a good example.

Worchel and Shebilske conclude their discussion on defense mechanisms by stating, "We live in a complex physical and social environment and sometimes it is difficult to adjust." Having an extra-marital affair adds to our already "stressed out" lives. "Pressures may build up slowly or we may need a temporary safety valve to help us cope with the difficulty. Defense mechanisms are safety valves that we all use. They redirect, reinterpret, or block out difficult situations and anxiety but they are seldom effective over an extended period." Not only are they seldom effective, they make the situation worse by extending its life and making it more complex.

CHOICE OR CHEAT

In ordinary life situations we find ourselves tantalized by the prospect of an affair. We can choose to persevere with our original choice to remain committed to our marriage, or we can choose to cheat. The choice we make subjects us to the consequences we face.

If we choose to pursue an affair it is usually because we are pursuing personal self-fulfillment. According to Marcus Lawah, there are three categories that perpetuate affairs for personal reasons or self-fulfillment. The first scenario is the single man/woman lifestyle. This is a lifestyle where the individual has chosen to be single. This category does not involve any extra-marital involvement because the participants are not obstructed by the marriage commitment. When they engage in a relationship they do not have anything to lose and there are no negative consequences, only fantasies. They are free.

The second scenario is where both the man and the woman in an affair are already committed in a marriage contract. Lawah considers this a social disease because this arrangement is a lie. Both individuals engage in an affair in the name of self-fulfillment. They are not cheating themselves but they are betraying their spouses, because they are breaking their marriage vows and commitment. Both individuals involved go back to their spouses carrying a mask of innocence. They believe that it is better to live with a secret than to live with miserable confessions.

In the third category one of the two involved in the affair is either acting out a choice or playing the cheat. The single individual is acting out on a choice and the married partner is playing the cheat. Lawah contends that both are liars and are seeking childish gratification.

Lawah concludes by asserting the perpetual human conflict. There is still the human ability to overcome problems against all odds for the sake of doing what is best for you.

You realize that your life is torn and uncertain. You are settling for less of a life, not only with your family but also with your lover. You continue to hang on and begin to justify and rationalize the situation to escape the pain and guilt. You exhibit defense mechanisms to help cope and escape from everything that weighs down on you. The consequences that you will face while you are making a conscious choice to remain committed to your marriage or cheat and betray your spouse as well as yourself and family will begin to manifest themselves and take a toll on you in many different ways.

Let's take a look at the effect that a decision to have an extra-marital affair will make on your emotional and physical well-being.

CHAPTER EIGHT

Symptoms, Signs and Signals

*"I wish people who have trouble communicating
would just shut up."*
Tom Lehrer

"We had seen the light at the end of the tunnel, and it was out."
John C. Clancy

"It's a rare person who wants to hear what he doesn't want to hear."
Dick Cavett

*"The most happy marriage I can imagine to myself would be the
union of a deaf man to a blind woman."*
Samuel Taylor Coleridge

SYMPTOMS

An affair is a sign of a need for help: an attempt to compensate for deficiencies in a person or a relationship, a warning that someone is suffering. The disintegration of your relationship comes to light long before you make any decisions to make changes.

Sheresky and Mannes paint the following scenario in their book, *Uncoupling: The Art of Coming Apart: A Guide to*

Sane Divorce, as a symptom to a bad marriage. Imagine a couple in a restaurant having dinner. They eat but they do not talk. They look, but not at each other. Their eyes and ears are turned toward a pair at the table opposite theirs: a man and a woman locked in each other's gaze, speaking softly, inaudibly, sometimes laughing together, holding each other's hands on the table.

The older, speechless couple shrivels inside. Were they ever like that? And if they were, what happened? These are, of course, markers of a dead marriage, a man and a woman who once thought they had it made and failed or refused to recognize the symptoms indicating that they hadn't.

This incident is an example of what Sheresky and Mannes believe might be the beginning of one very important symptom, the failure to recognize that there is a breakdown that has resulted in the failure of sex and the failure of communication. But this is the end, not the beginning. Having failed for many years to feel for each other, they are incapable of doing so. Their feelings have turned into either the mute hatred of the trapped or the desperate boredom of the habitual.

Perhaps you're having financial difficulties, severe business problems or professional failure. Sheresky and Mannes maintain that your spouse doesn't achieve the same kind of release in talking out his problems as you do. As a result, your spouse withdraws into a cocoon. What are the signals they missed along the way? Some very obvious ones would include a shared inability to agree on financial matters, like money, savings, and division of property. Or family matters like having children and raising them, or on personal matters, like the acceptance or rejection of each other's friends and relatives.

Sheresky and Mannes further contend that sexual dissatisfaction is another sign of a failing marriage. This problem could take the form of a slow withering of shared desire, or—even worse—a greater sexual need in one partner than the other. To turn toward a person who does not turn toward you can become unbearable, leading ultimately to a search for satisfaction outside the home for one spouse and the silent lack of fulfillment for the other.

Sheresky and Mannes maintain that communication can also take on a doomed feeling of dread for married couples. For example, saying the wrong thing at the wrong time, such as, "Your mother's coming over this weekend," can spoil one's spouse's sex-appetite. Many couples find it difficult to communicate with each other and often fail to realize the need of one or both partners to talk and to be taken seriously. Professional or financial failure is a threat to anyone's well being and leaves us feeling vulnerable and drained. This puts a strain on the relationship because one partner is in a weakened condition and cannot communicate his feelings.

Sheresky and Mannes assert that many couples cannot talk about sex, about what they expect in the relationship about sex or what they are not satisfied with. They chose to not talk altogether. This inability to communicate sexual needs or frustrations can work against mutual sexual satisfaction. A verbal confrontation and shouting match regarding many issues in a marriage is a common temporary release of frustration, but deep seated hidden dissatisfactions concerning sex that are not expressed are the most harmful because they are silent, repressive, guild-laden and misunderstood.

The silence of non-confrontation regarding sexual dissatisfaction or any other issue in marriage negates attempts to have marriage become successful. Some couples will not discuss their feelings openly because they are not comfortable and they cannot remain honest. They feel that being honest would interfere and cloud the issues and that their concerns or frustrations would become criticized or due further damage. However, they contradict their attempt to find happiness in the relationship. Some feel that total honesty can be more dangerous than deception. Only when you have the ability to understand, sympathize and truly empathize with your spouse or put yourself in his or her shoes can productive communication become successful.

This misunderstanding leads to the feeling that you can function better without your partner than with him. It is not a good situation when you would usually rather be alone or with somebody else than with him. It is not a good situation when you think that your children would profit from the absence of their father.

If you find it difficult to discuss your intimate feelings with your spouse then it is obvious that the relationship is suffering in many other areas. For example, a relationship is deteriorating if both partners have considerably less fun together than they used to. It is truly hopeless when neither spouse has any fun at all.

Additionally, relationships disintegrate and become corroded if you allow or nurture neurotic behavior from your partner. For example, does he talk on the telephone incessantly, conducting business while he is at home and interrupt dinner? Are you an enabler? For example, do you accept this behavior as part of what is required to be successful financially so you never protest even though it is a major source of your dissatisfaction? Enablers assist and sanction neurotic behavior but they secretly despise it and hold their discontentment to themselves and ultimately this results in their frustration. Behavior such as compulsive gambling or alcoholism and compulsive spending are examples of neurotic behavior. Perhaps you enable each other to remain in your strange worlds rather than accept or search out workable alternatives.

Only two responses to such behavior make sense: Do something about the destructive behavior, or realize that it will not get any better. Maybe you are desperate for professional help but at the same time you realize that if you seek help you will be forced to make a decision and opt for an alternative that will change the comfortable existence that has allowed you to survive up to this point. If you decide to do something about your situation then you may have to come face to face with the realization that your relationship may be over.

Eventually, if you desire a better quality relationship or if you want to end the relationship, you will be faced with the decision of how to confront your husband about your dissatisfactions. Perhaps the intensification of the hurts, the feelings of rejection, and the costs of the relationship may have reached a point where you do not want the relationship anymore. Perhaps you see the reality of the problems in the relationship and realize that they cannot be remedied.

Rarely does anyone consider what action she will have to take if she takes the initiative to separate. You will have to evaluate and examine the vital factors such as costs, emotionally, socially and financially, of ending your relationship before the ultimate leap. They are more important than the attitudes of family or friends. Unfortunately, these factors are often ignored. In the two crucial human decisions—to marry and to divorce—knowledge and reason play the smallest part. Most people do not want to face them. The disintegration of a relationship is almost entirely ignored until it is too late, because the failure of a marriage feels like a personal failure to the couple and may even represent, to them, the failure of their society.

SIGNS

In his book, *How to Get Out of An Unhappy Marriage Relationship: The Intelligent Woman's and Man's Guide to the Marriage Break,* Dr. Eugene Walder lists several signs that will enable you to realize when you would be better off without your spouse.

Are you tired, fatigued, and tense? Suppressing your feelings can drain your energy. Pay attention to your body. It may be telling you about something about your marriage. But—you'll need a clean bill of health from your doctor before you can begin to diagnose physical symptoms as expressions of your unhappiness.

Do you get headaches when you're around your spouse? Have you considered that your marriage may be a "big headache" to you?

Do you get "the shakes" when you're with your spouse? You may be shaking with bottled-up rage.

Do you feel apprehensive about returning home? What scene are you picturing in your mind? Certainly not your loving spouse greeting you with a drink.

Do you often feel irritable? If you do, you're angry about something. Try to identify the source of your anger. Monitor your feelings when you're with your spouse. Does what your spouse talks about irritate you? Do you experience a welling-up of anger? Do you suppress your feelings because of guilt or fear of disapproval or fear of loss of love?

Do you get a sinking feeling in the pit of your stomach when you hear your spouse's footsteps? If you do, your marriage may be going under.

Do you feel lonely and empty even when you are with your spouse? Isn't this a sign that your marriage isn't fulfilling your needs?

Do you constantly pick on your spouse about little things? Somehow you can't seem to stop yourself. Perhaps you wish you had made a better pick when you got married.

Do you say things you don't mean when you're drinking? You may be sorry later. But it's not the alcohol speaking. It's you. Alcohol can be a potent truth serum because it relaxes one's inhibitions.

Are you afraid of displeasing your spouse? If you are, how can you express your real feelings? You can't! You have to dam them up. That damns your marriage.

Do you take the frustrations of your marriage out on your children? If you do, you're taking it out on innocent bystanders.

Do you manage to spend a lot of time away from home? Are you trying to get away from it all?

Do you feel envious and cynical when you see a loving couple? Would you really like to be in their shoes, your "style" uncramped by your marriage?

Are your children the center of your life? If they are, your marriage is off center. Your children will leave home, but your spouse will stay. He should be the center of your marriage for you.

How is your sex life? Do you look forward to it with anticipation or dread? Your sex life is a barometer of whether your marriage is fair or foul.

Do you fantasize about having an affair with someone else? Are you trying to escape from an unpleasant reality?

Do both of you constantly argue about the children? If you do, your energy may be misdirected, and your feelings too. What is it you can't say to each other?

Are you unfaithful? Is it because you believe variety is the spice of life, or simply that your marriage is too unpleasant to stomach?

What is your unconscious trying to tell you about your marriage? Do you have strange and cryptic dreams?

Do you see a new bride and groom and say to yourself, "Damn fools!" Are you talking to yourself about yourself?

DANGER SIGNALS

Perhaps you have decided that you would rather engage in an extra-marital affair rather than go through the pains of professional marriage counseling, separation and divorce or face up to your own short comings. According to Bonnie Eaker Weil, Ph.D, in her book, *Adultery: The Forgivable Sin: Healing the Inherited Patterns of Betrayal in Your Family*, listed below are a few "Danger Signals" that you should take into consideration if you elect to go this route or you have the inkling that your husband is having an affair.

There are obvious tip-offs: hang-up calls and whispered conversations; strange charges on the phone bill or credit card; the uncharacteristic whiff of alcohol or an unfamiliar fragrance; diminished interest in sex; or increased interest in sex.

Sometimes, though, the evidence can be subtler. Is your wife spending a lot more time away from home—on business trips, at meetings, nights out with the girls? Are lunch hours very leisurely?

Is she going to work earlier and coming home later? When you call, does the office have trouble tracking your mate down?

Do sales conferences or evening classes seem to last longer than they used to?

When at home, is your mate restless? Does she suddenly spend an extraordinary amount of time doing "good deeds" such as running your errands for you or become more generous than usual as if to compensate for guilt?

When you are together, do you find yourself talking less and watching television more?

Has your spouse suddenly discovered a boundless desire to work out at the gym or a new dedication to a diet?

Has your spouse changed an accustomed way of dressing, wearing sexier lingerie?

Has your spouse suddenly tried a makeover previously resisted—getting contacts, wearing short skirts, letting hair or nails grow long?

Has he gotten a hairpiece or implants? Has she streaked her hair?

Has sex changed in any of the following ways? Do you make love more or less often than usual? Are new techniques suddenly appearing or being asked for? Has foreplay changed? The afterglow? Has your spouse stopped using sexual endearments or pet names?

Has your spouse become very secretive about credit-card slips? Does your spouse check the answering service or the caller ID first thing upon entering the house? Is your partner provoking more fights or being more belligerent when you argue?

Has the level of fault finding risen?

Do your children show signs of stress: clinging, nightmares, bedwetting, and aggressive behavior in school, extreme shyness, or hyperactivity?

Having fallen out of love still leaves decisions to be made. There are three possible choices: (a) to make a move toward getting out of the relationship, to separate or divorce; (b) to try through counseling or other means to rekindle the love that once existed; (c) to resign oneself totally to a non-intimate relationship. Reasons for staying in such a marriage may include any of the following: one's stage in the life cycle, religious convictions, guilt, pity, finances, feelings of failure (which may be greater if there were previous divorces), children, health, or commitment to the institution of marriage.

Coming to grips with these decisions or to have an extramarital affair is a life-altering decision. It is not merely an event in one's life; it is a process with many facets. Emotions, behaviors and thoughts are all involved and there are many signs and symptoms of its onset before you come to these stages. Dissolution usually occurs after some emptiness, disorder or turbulence has been in existence in the relationship for some time. A relationship may have broken down to the point where you do nothing with, or say almost nothing to, each other. You still, however, reside together, as in an empty-shell marriage even though few, if any, emotional bonds exist between you and your husband.

CHAPTER NINE

Does Change Scare You?

"Remember that a kick in the ass is a step forward."
Unknown

"Life is what happens when you are making other plans."
John Lennon

"The art of living is more like wrestling than dancing."
Marcus Aurelius

"Everything changes but the avant garde."
Paul Valery

CAN YOU PULL THE PLUG?

Many psychologists believe that fear is one of the greatest blocks to self-fulfillment. Afraid of failure, most people tend to follow the safe path. Unfortunately, since each person is unique, the same path is not right for all. Some people "conform" to society's demands at an enormous cost—losing sight of their real needs their real selves. In a relationship, this means too many women try to force themselves into whatever society defines as a good wife. In the end, they usually are unable to live up to this standard and blame themselves or others. The result is an unhappy relationship or marriage. There is no magic way to ensure that every marriage will be successful, or even that every woman, given a choice, will become the best person she can be, with or without marriage.

Dr. Walder contends that an unhappy marriage can be tied up in knots of hopelessness and despair that defy untying. When you feel that your marriage is going nowhere, you may have to make a decision. Divorce is a bold solution. How willing are you to consider it?

More than half the marriages in this country end in divorce. Divorce is traumatic; a good deal of trauma is the trauma of change. Leaving the protection of marriage is traumatic for any adult, but it can be the beginning of a new life.

Dr. Walder believes that the outcome depends upon you and your expectations. If you expect to have an open wound for the rest of your life, then you will. If you expect the wound to heal, then it will, and you'll be stronger than you were before.

Divorce can make you feel that you are not living up to some of your expectations such as the values of commitment and responsibility. You are always thinking that it may not be fair or wise to break up your family and remove your children from their good father (This assumes that abuse and addiction are not factors). You constantly question if your reasons to divorce are not selfish because your marriage is not exciting or fulfilling for you. You wonder if seeking happiness and emotional and sexual fulfillment will make a better life for your and your children. You constantly rehash all of this in your mind and ask yourself if you are willing to take the risks that involve getting a divorce. These are all very important considerations.

You cannot find the truth about yourself without suffering some anxiety. Ending a marriage is not easy. You will find that it is necessary to become aware of everything that surrounds you such as the issues mentioned earlier and how your choices and decisions will effect your children, if you have any, and your future. It probably will be necessary for you to change your behavior in a real and particular manner. One thing you will need is to have a positive support group of trusted friends that you can rely on to listen to what you are planning. You'll need all the help you can get.

If it isn't possible for you to grow within the limits of a satisfying marriage, then it is preferable to end the marriage in order to stimulate your emotional and psychological growth.

Change brings many ramifications. If a storm destroys a forest, the land undergoes a change. However, the trees will regrow if they receive the proper nutrients. In the same way, you can "regrow" your world after a divorce. You will need to make an assessment of what "essential nutrients" you will need for this growth. People have a natural tendency to grow and mature and to realize their potential as human beings. They learn to become independent; communicate with each other; give and receive love; assume responsibility; understand themselves and others; be creative, and take risks. Growth begins at birth and ends only at death. Children say, "When I grow up...." Yet, if we're fully aware of our lives, we never stop growing. Growth is a lifelong process. We never outgrow the need to grow. Although it sounds peculiar, true security is found in change.

NUTRIENTS FOR CHANGE

A human being requires several nutrients in order to grow emotionally. If you decide to change your life and divorce your spouse, these same nutrients will be necessary for you to continue to grow and be successful in your life. Before you initiate a divorce, ask yourself if your marriage is lacking in any of these nutrients. If you are leaving your marriage for someone, can he supply these nutrients, if in fact you need anyone to supply them?

Dr. Walder contends that your marriage should be a principle source of these nutrients:

LOVE—Define what you believe love is. You will know if your spouse or lover feels it for you or if you feel it for him. Love is sometimes defined as seeking the highest good in another person.

UNDERSTANDING—Are you compatible with each other? Do you suit each other's needs? Are you sympathetic to each other? Do you appreciate each other? Are you sensitive to each other's wants and needs?

ACCEPTANCE—Can you unconditionally accept your partner? Especially for what he is and what he can be? Is your relationship agreeable and pleasing? Do you feel desirable, lovable, sexy, smart, funny, and interesting with your partner? When was the last time both of you used these adjectives to describe each other?

RESPECT—Do you hold your partner in high esteem? Do you both treat each other with affection and respect?

TRUST—Can you confide in your partner without feeling judged or self-conscious or compromised? Would your partner embarrass you in an argument and bring up a confidence or secret that you share, possibly about a shortcoming that you might have?

COMMUNICATION—Can you relate to your partner? Can you get through to each other? Are you both active talkers and listeners during your discussions?

APPROVAL—Do you endorse and accept each other? Do you have each other's "seal of approval"?

LAUGHTER—If there's no laughter in your marriage, it's no laughing matter.

EMOTIONAL SUPPORT—Are you there to defend and support each other whenever you need each other? Can you count on your partner without fear of being let down?

FRIENDSHIP—Do you have a mutual affection and regard for each other?

SEXUAL SATISFACTION—Do you meet each other's sexual desires and expectations? You should not feel guilty or inhibited when asking for or giving sex.

UNREALISTIC EXPECTATIONS

Before you decide to take the leap and divorce, take a moment to assess your thoughts and make sure you are not having unrealistic expectations. Maintaining a marriage is hard work. Unrealistic expectations of marriage can make it difficult for any marriage to succeed in real life. By seeking personal happiness and self-fulfillment we have expectations of our husband that he cannot fulfill all of the time and we would be thoughtless and self-centered to expect and demand that he did.

A couple lives with a sort of sixth sense of what their partner thrives on and what they contribute to the health of the marriage. Couples usually can relate to each other without words or gestures. For example, many women know when their husbands are thinking about having sex with them by the subtle nuances that they have come to know as a sort of code that they share with their husbands. Inevitably, however, the experience of marriage falls short of our expectations, especially if our expectations are unrealistic. When your relationship falls below your expectations, you feel that you are deprived of one or more nutrients. When you realize that this is happening to you, be aware that you have to act on what is happening to your relationship in order to repair it.

When you are in the process of determining if divorce is your best choice you will have to make a choice and act on that choice. Many women do not want to act. Acting means making a change and change is not readily accepted. You will have to admit that your marriage is not living up to your expectations, and women often choose to suppress this realization. Suppression turns into anger and anger leads to arguing and depression. You may find it difficult to admit that you are unhappy.

When you become consistently unhappy, you lose your enthusiasm for life. You lack the intensity, inspiration, and stamina to deal with life's challenges and responsibilities. Life will be tedious and monotonous, and it will be difficult to accomplish anything. You won't be able to meet the emotional and sexual needs of your partner.

ARE YOU GOOD FOR EACH OTHER?

Good is an inherent quality that we use to qualify our feelings. Good in a relationship signifies an attractive, complimentary promising or favorable quality. A good relationship is one worth attaining and is beneficial because it is complimentary and it expresses our approval of each other. Having a good relationship is having a relationship that is satisfactory or adequate. Sanctioning and confirming your partner as a growing maturing person and realizing your own as well as your partner's capabilities is essential to evaluating whether or not you are good for each other. The possibility that you have outgrown each other is always a consideration. If you or your partner has ceased growing because you cannot help each other to be the best they can be by realizing their potential, then it may be possible that you simply are not meant for each other.

DENIAL

You may begin to deny that your marriage is imperfect or rationalize that there are really no perfect marriages. You may even begin to question real happiness and if it would ever be possible to attain it. You may feel that you would be shirking your commitment and responsibilities if you did not try to make your marriage work. You may have difficulty conceiving that your investment in your marriage might end. You might begin to persuade yourself that you are really not that unhappy. You believe your marriage was a serious, conscientious commitment and therefore you must try to make it work. If you allow yourself to realize that you are unhappy, you will have to act on your emotions and feelings, and this may be difficult for you.

When you refuse to accept the facts, you enter into the denial stage. Even though everything points to a serious breakdown of communication and a realization that you cannot meet the needs of your partner and vise versa, you still want to rationalize that everything is OK. You rationalize that all marriages have their ups and downs. You should be asking yourself if your marriage is more down than up.

The situation becomes even worse if you believe that your partner will change if they are confronted. After all, they have promised to do so in the past. How many times has this promise been made—and broken? Yes, maybe people can change, but look at the statistics. Usually you will find that optimism in this regard is not justified.

Maybe you believe that a good marriage takes the bad with the good. You rationalize that if the bad and good were split 50-50, your marriage would be ten times better than it is. Half of the time you were satisfied with your relationship and half of the time you were not satisfied. Wake up! This is not an equitable scenario. Sometimes, in a good marriage, you will give of yourself ninety percent and some days you will only contribute ten percent. The thought that you must be flexible in marriage must be taken into consideration. However, taking all the burdens of the relationship too often or all of the time is simply avoiding the inevitable.

Maybe you believe that sex isn't everything. That's true, it's not. Dr. Walder believes that if you have to constantly reassure yourself on this one, there's a good chance that sex isn't anything in your marriage.

All marriages go through crisis and good marriages have many ups and downs. There is no such thing as perfection. The real issue is to ask yourself how long your crisis has been going on and if you are afraid of becoming another divorce statistic?

WOULD YOU BE HAPPY WITH SOMEONE ELSE?

We all reveal different sides of ourselves to different people. With some people we can be more ourselves than with others. We are less defensive and don't have to keep our guard up. These people bring out the best in us.

Dr. Walder maintains that you should ask yourself the following questions:

> Do you ever have the feeling that you can be more yourself with someone else other than your spouse?

> Do you feel cheated because you have to hold yourself back with the person you should be closest to?

> People in denial begin asking themselves questions like this: Why look for trouble? Who needs it? Aren't you happy if you think you're happy? Why not leave well enough alone?

Paula was one such person. She had been experiencing bouts with migraine headaches and always felt nervous tension in the pit of her stomach. She was trying to juggle working part-time and caring for her two children, ages seven and four. She couldn't afford to pursue her career and pay for child-care. She was also having an affair with Andrew.

Paula and her husband, Jeff, had been in "limbo" for nearly six out of the seven years they had been married. They very rarely communicated with each other intimately or verbally. When Paula became pregnant with their son, she and Jeff decided the best thing to do would be to marry. They initially had a great deal of support and financial help from their parents, as well as loving childcare, but in the last four years they both lost their parents.

Paula and Jeff inherited two new cars, a moderately new ranch home and a substantial stock portfolio. With this windfall Paula was able to pursue her marketing career and eventually go to work in a prestigious downtown advertising agency. Jeff continued the family's stationery business, which he and Paula worked on together before the children were born. Jeff was pre-occupied just about twenty-four hours a day and seven days a week. This led to a great deal of unrest in the marriage, and Paula's decision to work didn't help the situation.

Andrew, the head of her department, was a single, attractive man-about-town. He took Paula to every fashionable restaurant and boutique in the city. Often she spent the night at his posh uptown apartment. Andrew was her peer in every respect and he more than satisfied her mentally, physically, emotionally and sexually. He accepted and respected her, and she could trust him implicitly. They were best friends and could communicate and understand each other. He helped her with the children and her children grew to love Andrew because he was more available than their father was. He always cheered her on to more independence

In contrast, Paula's relationship with her husband was non-existent. Their only mutual pursuit was the success of the stationery business, and they had little time left over for intimacy or to develop any kind of relationship. Jeff was pre-occupied with the success of the business, and he made it perfectly clear that his efforts aimed at success were paramount for the survival of the family.

Andrew proposed that Paula leave Jeff and marry him. She became irritable at the thought of tearing up her children's lives for her own gratification. She was so deprived of a relationship with her husband that she became frustrated, angry and, most of all, unhappy and depressed. She denied that this was happening to her and tried to rationalize that most couples experience this kind of crisis in their marriage.

Paula and Jeff constantly argued about the children, and she experienced a great deal of apprehension when she had to go home. She was always angry and took her frustration out on the children by shouting at them. She felt lonely and empty without Andrew. Jeff constantly picked on her for little things.

Paula continually denied her unhappiness and could not admit that she did not love Jeff. She was avoiding the situation by staying away from home. She was too insecure to leave.

Paula was in denial. She was comfortable with her marriage and she refused to accept that she could not communicate with Jeff and Jeff could not meet her needs. The idea of ending her marriage scared Paula more than any other thought. It was difficult for Paula to admit that she did not love Jeff, but this feeling would not go away. Finally, she grew stronger and more independent and eventually decided to divorce Jeff.

FACING THE TRUTH

Admitting to your husband that he does not fulfill you sexually or that you would prefer to live alone is a scary proposition. You would have to admit that you couldn't stand him to touch you or that you could no longer trust him.

If you couldn't articulate your feelings, you would have to suppress them. However, this unhappy feeling would not go away. You would be constantly reminded of your despondency because you would be living with your husband. Masking your true feelings would cause you to become irritable, tired and depressed. You may also experience problems such as tension and headaches.

If you revealed your negative thoughts about your husband to him it would mean the end of your marriage. You would have to move on. Perhaps you would lose financial security, your circle of friends and your status and respect in your community. You would believe that you are jumping out of the frying pan and into the fire. If you left, you would have to reduce your standard of living or relocate and uproot your children.

In effect you are in a marriage that has no room for personal growth. Marriage takes up too big a part of your life to spend it with a spouse who makes you unhappy. By denying your misery, you don't have to act. And if you don't have to act, then you don't have to worry about finding someone else, or failing in another relationship, or finding yourself worse off than you were before.

TAKING RISKS

Having an affair means that something is wrong with your marriage. But being aware that your marriage is unhappy and unfulfilling won't do you a bit of good until you make a conscious effort to make a change and do something about your unhappiness. Perhaps you are vacillating because you are aware of all the risks involved in ending your marriage.

Getting a divorce means that you will have to face many changes such as living alone and having full or part-time custody of your children. Part-time parenting means seeing your children only on weekends and not experiencing their day to day lives. On the other hand, if you retain full custody you may be forced to shoulder all of the responsibility alone for the care of the children. Divorce also means having to support yourself or relocating to another city and facing the unknown. Perhaps you should ask yourself, What would I become? Will ending my marriage be an overwhelming risk?

Suppose you decided to end your marriage. Try to visualize the future and imagine yourself in certain situations such as those described above. You will probably realize from this exercise that your survival is not at stake. If you could be confident that your life would be better for yourself and your children, would you wait one minute before going ahead with divorce proceedings? Be honest with yourself. Do you genuinely believe you would choose to stay?

Change is difficult for many women and divorce is a major life change. Engaging in an extra-marital affair may mean that you will have to face the change and challenge of divorce. In the process leading up to this decision you will vacillate between your safe and secure marriage and an uncertain future. You must evaluate the divorce process carefully before you decide to dissolve your marriage. Change is a process and this process will involve anxiety and fear. You will experience growing pains and you will need to make an assessment of what you will need to grow and find security. If you decide to change your life and divorce, these needs or nutrients will be necessary for you to continue to grow and be successful. In this process check to make sure that you don't have unrealistic expectations of your husband and make sure that you definitely are not compatible with him and that you would be happy with another man. Sometimes facing the truth is difficult and when you are in denial you will not be able to make this proposed change. You will have to admit that you are not fulfilled and you will have to accept that you will move on. You need to understand what this change will cost you and decide if you can take the risk.

We do not need a crystal ball to anticipate our future. We determine our own future. The future is not fated. Choose to regress into doom and you abandon your responsibility for your own life. Don't be afraid of the future because it means that you are afraid of yourself. If you cannot get out of an unhappy marriage then you don't have the confidence to believe in yourself. You need the conviction to assure yourself that you can make the future turn out all right. The choices you make today affect the quality of your life tomorrow.

CHAPTER TEN

Losing and Grieving

"Show me a good loser and I'll show you an idiot."
Leo Durocher
"Show me a good loser and I'll show you a loser."
Unknown

ENDING AN AFFAIR

If you decide to break off the affair possibly because you feel guilty about betraying your spouse or you feel the children would experience life altering psychological problems and would not adjust, or maybe you realize you truly love your husband, you will go through a transition.

Your realization that your affair is over—even if you were the one to initiate the break-up—can require an adjustment process. How you adapt to your new lifestyle can depend on how you react to various stages in the regretting or adjusting process. You could begin by feeling indifferent or apathetic, or you might refuse to believe that your relationship is finished. You could spend your days in a state of listlessness, or you could be experiencing a great deal of anxiety and restlessness.

If you had a strong emotional attachment to your lover, you could begin to experience desperate longing for him, as well as anger and guilt. You could become even angrier with your spouse and children and withdraw from any social ties. Loneliness might result, and you might feel even more desperate to be part of the life of your lover or have some contact with him. You will miss his companionship and how he compensated for what was missing in your marriage.

Who will replace this emotional loss? Will you seek comfort from your spouse or will you begin another affair? If you decide to try another affair, you might have many unresolved emotional issues that you must untangle before you do anything, including divorcing your spouse. Psychologists stress that emotional closeness with others and relationships of mutuality are "vital factors" in your overall well-being. If you cannot experience consistent emotional closeness, perhaps you have underlying unresolved issues, which were discussed earlier, that must be addressed in counseling before you go any further.

You might then begin to form new expectations of your spouse, even if they seemingly have no purpose. For example...you might become even more dependent on your spouse and make more foolish decisions. You might be trying to face yourself for the very first time and determine and evaluate what is lacking within.

Finally, you might then begin to accept your shortcomings as well as your husband's, and welcome new, more profound experiences in your life.

If your affair was a secret, you will not have comfort and support from anyone unless you confided in someone during the affair. You may want to talk with a professional therapist, since the presence and advice of a person you can confide in is an important part of your recovery.

You might experience withdrawal from the hectic life that you have been used to coping with so effectively. You might wonder how you ever managed such a complex life given the fact that many people have difficulty coping with marriage plus children and a job. If you have become accustomed to thriving on chaos and excitement, you might experience dismay, boredom or confusion when your life suddenly becomes less demanding.

Maybe you were more dependent on your lover than you realized. You were able to share your dissatisfactions with your marriage with him and gained special approval for being yourself. Your lover accepted you and affirmed you as a person. You were his "special angel." If you cannot find a non-sexual outlet for this need, such as a friend, therapist, or your spouse, you may find yourself regretting the break-up of your affair.

You may feel inadequate with your daily life because you always had someone to share all your little ups and downs with, someone you could count on to comfort you. Your lover shared your pleasure and your pain. Ideally, your husband should also fill this role.

Your identity might suffer because you never realized how dependent you were on your lover for your self-concept. Let's discuss some reasons why you would end an affair.

FULFILLMENT

Perhaps you have come to the realization that the reason you began the affair in the first place has been fulfilled or satisfied. Although not a healthy reason, maybe you were having the affair in retaliation for something your spouse did to you. Once you finally felt that you had inflicted enough pain and agony, you quit the affair.

Perhaps the affair began because it provided you with a great deal of fun and excitement. If you have matured, you might now desire a more stable, productive relationship. Perhaps your marriage fulfills this need and you no longer find your lover's boyish charm so enticing.

The sex you found so provocative and taboo in the beginning is finally becoming boring and comfortable, as if you and your lover have been married for twenty years. You can experience this at home in a stable relationship without all of the hassle, deceit and potential upheaval.

You feel that your lover is no longer passionate and exciting and no longer makes you feel attractive and important. Instead you feel that you might be able to work things out at home and cultivate a trusting, loving relationship with your spouse, with some effort. You realize that the payoff for your effort will be worth far more than any pleasure you receive from someone in whom you have invested little time, especially since you will still experience all the uncertainties that accompany an affair.

In all likelihood you have realized that the risk you were thrilled with in the beginning of the affair will cost too much in terms of your health and self-respect. You believe that, when you weigh all the facts, the affair is simply not worth the risk. You are headed in the path of self-destruction with far-reaching potential consequences to yourself and your family. In other words, you do not want to be a victim of circumstances you have created.

If you were having an affair with an old flame from college or high school, or even a former spouse, you might be trying to recapture idealized memories of a lost romance to rekindle an old flame. It was exciting to feel so young and uninhibited for awhile, but you now realize that your old fantasies are nothing more than school-girl whims.

Perhaps you went through a phase in which you concluded that you wanted a more meaningful life. You realized that your life lacked substance. However, you find now that what you truly want to achieve in your life is to remain married in a relationship that is built on working through difficult times and relying on your spouse.

Affairs happen for various reasons. It may be that your affair no longer meets the need that made it so important in the beginning. You no longer feel that you are loved, needed or understood. Gone is the feeling that you have a special friendship, or that the affair gives you a better sense of freedom or independence. Perhaps the intellectual stimulation has become stale or boring and is no longer a vital part of the relationship. Maybe you no longer share intimate conversation or share new experiences that give you the feeling that you are experiencing a new meaningful adventure.

All of these reasons can apply to ending your affair. You must weigh the potential consequences, good or bad, and come to a decision with which you will be comfortable living.

Take my friend Marsha, for example. Married fifteen years with no children, she was as comfortable in her marriage as she was in her old, broken-in Nikes. Then one Christmas she met Miguel at a friend's party. (Her husband, who had the flu, stayed home.) Miguel was from Spain. Five years her junior, he was handsome, charming and shrouded in all the exotic mystery that Marsha had always associated with Latin countries.

Marsha's affair with Miguel crept up on her when she least expected it. She thought that she could maintain a friendship with him, meeting for lunch or coffee to discuss her favorite Spanish artists and Spanish history. Their get-togethers felt exciting, adventurous, and a little thrilling, even naughty. Then one night, when Miguel stopped as he was driving her home from a lecture on Madrid, they made love in his car. Marsha had never felt anything so thrilling or intriguing as making love with Miguel. He called her endearments in Spanish and even sang to her afterward and recited poetry. Her husband never did any of that!

After a few months of a clandestine, passionate affair with Miguel, Marsha was convinced that she would never be able to give him up. He made her feel revitalized and exuberant. How lucky she was, she thought, to have found such a glamorous, kind, intelligent man who was so enamored of her that he brought her a red rose every time they met. On the other hand, she was lucky if Bob, her husband, remembered to buy her flowers on their anniversary.

After a year of this secret affair, Marsha left Bob for Miguel and moved into the Spaniard's apartment. It was tidy and colorful, as it always was whenever she visited, and Miguel was as vivacious as ever. Marsha felt a little guilty over leaving Bob, who had wept when she told him her decision. She had never seen him weep before. Still, she was certain she had found someone who understood her and appreciated her for who she was.

Over the next year, however, Marsha found that her relationship with Miguel had changed. They no longer went out together very often, and Miguel seemed to prefer sitting at home drinking beer and watching soccer on TV to singing, quoting poets or discussing European history and politics. In fact, they spoke much less often to each other than they had before she had moved in. The roses stopped coming. The apartment was no longer tidy unless she tidied it herself. Most amazing of all to Marsha, Miguel seemed to have the same annoying habits that Bob had had. He clipped his toenails in the kitchen and left used underwear in the bathroom. (At least Bob had only left towels on the floor.) Miguel was still pleasant and charming, but he also seemed more distant, less interested in her. Sex was still exciting and passionate, but Marsha noticed that Miguel did not always want to do what she asked him to, and their lovemaking was beginning to feel less varied, less spontaneous.

One night, when she came home after a grueling day at work, Miguel met her at the door, furious that she did not have dinner waiting for him. They got into a heated discussion about equality, with Miguel insisting he was not a sexist, just hungry. Even though Miguel soon calmed down and apologized, Marsha had already begun to wonder whether or not she had made a mistake. What had happened to her wonderful, captivating affair?

What happened was this: Marsha had experienced a romantic courtship at the beginning of the affair. As she thought about the past, she recalled that Bob had also courted her passionately, if not exotically. But she had also experienced a long marriage with Bob, which included lots of low moments. Her first year with Miguel had been the intoxicating rush of courtship; her second year was shaping up to be another comfortable-old-Nikes marriage. She wondered if Bob would take her back.

CHAPTER ELEVEN

The Test

"Love is an obsessive delusion that is cured by marriage."
Dr. Karl Bowman

*"Men are like the earth and we are the moon; we turn always one
side to them, and they think there is no other,
because they don't see it—but there is."*
Olive Schreiner

WHERE ARE WE GOING?

If you are having an extra-marital affair, or are contemplating one, examine this chapter thoroughly. It is important to clarify the expectations of each partner in the relationship about the future and to share similar goals and plans for the affair. It is also important to work out certain strategies and the ground rules of issues such as secrecy, exclusivity and commitment. This test will help you jog your mind to think of things that can help you determine if you are compatible with the man with whom you wish to have an extra-marital affair. Or, you can use this test with your husband to help you iron out possible contentious sources or problems that have caused you to be dissatisfied with your marriage. Compatibility in a relationship is important to its success. Compatibility enables you to decide if you will be mutually tolerant or are well-suited for each other.

You may decide to use this test to revitalize your relationship with your spouse, or you may use this test to decide if you will be successful if you decide to leave your spouse. This test would also be helpful to a young couple thinking about marriage.

The terms lover/spouse, significant other, partner or him used in this chapter include your husband or the man with whom you are having the extra-marital affair or are planning to have the extra-marital affair and do not merit separate treatment.

When you initiate self-examination, you become responsible and accountable for your actions and you are better able to meet the consequences of your choices. This is the beginning of your move toward taking responsibility for yourself. When you do this, you will begin to define your relationship inside or outside of marriage or both. Making your choice clear by defining its potential, contributes to a better understanding of the person to whom you wish to commit yourself to as your significant other. "Significant other" in this case implies the person with whom you feel you are at your best, regardless of your limitations or achievements. You can outline your needs and expectations as well as your partner's and make important decisions to define your relationship. In doing this you will be better able to assess if this person is the right mate for you and if you both will have a successful relationship. You will be better able to live with your choice and protect yourself emotionally, physically, mentally and financially.

You must realize that there are no guarantees, but in doing this personal assessment of your needs and likes and dislikes to determine compatibility you won't be entering into this relationship wearing blinders. You will be thoughtfully and consciously weighing the potential of the relationship and the consequences of your choice. By taking control over your decisions you are acting in your own best interest and taking full responsibility for your actions.

In considering an extra-marital relationship, or whether or not you wish to divorce or remain married to your husband, it is necessary to understand the roles of family, society, cultural expectations and religion. Do not discount the significance of these major factors in your life. For example, ethnic men in certain groups are steeped in cultural traditions and have set ideas on the "place" of women. Can you live with that?

Define for yourself exactly what this type of commitment demands of you and seek answers no matter if the relationship is an extra-marital affair or marriage or if you are contemplating divorce. In doing this, you and your lover or spouse will help define exactly what your mutual and collective view of life will be and give you a deeper knowledge into both your expectations.

Uncovering and examining the facts can prevent a great deal of grief. Ask yourself exactly how important and necessary the answers to the questions you will be asked in this test are to your well-being. Keep in mind the consequences of continued frustration when your most significant needs are not met. Remember, when you cannot achieve satisfaction in a relationship or become unhappy because your needs in many areas are not met, you ultimately become frustrated; then anger, resentment, and outrage usually follow. Eventually, if your partner fails to satisfy your needs for affection, sex, attention, acceptance, approval, reassurance, praise or any other emotional requirement, it could be a major source of frustration and result in a breakdown of your relationship.

RULES

Take a few days to go through the following list of questions. It would be helpful to write your responses down and refer to them at a later date. You might want to take the test two times with your lover or husband, depending on how you wish to use the test. A calm, relaxed, safe and removed atmosphere, free of such distractions as children and phone calls, is the most conducive to a truthful, useful set of answers.

Do not interrupt him when it is his turn to answer any given question. Let him answer each question fully. Although many of the questions may result in yes/no answers, hopefully the questions will provoke an in depth conversation into the issues that are raised. Answer each question ONE AT A TIME. Give him your undivided attention. It would be helpful to know your answer ahead of time, so you should take it alone before you take it with him.

Don't be afraid to disagree. In fact, agree to disagree or simply disagree, but do not fight over your personal differences regarding the issues in question. When couples fight the main reason is always based on self-estimation or one-sided bias and second-guessing. For example, some disagreements are not about the issue at hand, but on the individuals' self-estimation or what they perceive is correct. Couples must clarify their reason for upset first and exchange opinions on the issue that they are arguing about. Don't turn a deaf ear on your lover. This refusal to hear what the individual is trying to say only alienates him because you want to control the argument so you do not reveal your true feelings. Perhaps you want to protect yourself or your lover from what you perceive is hurtful. However, deafness in a relationship will take its toll. Realize that differences are necessary and enriching to any relationship. Every day of your future life together will not be comfortable, and you will not always be able to agree, but you should be able to communicate your differences and your opinions.

Do not give ultimatums nor give into any of them. If you come to a deadlock put the question aside for future consideration. Remember you want a partner whom you can relate to as an equal, intellectually and emotionally.

Expect this from your husband or lover. Be truthful. If you are to accomplish success with this test or in your relationship you must trust each other enough to be totally open and vulnerable, while making no judgments about each other.

The questions in this "test" are not all-inclusive. Hopefully, they will prompt more in-depth scrutiny, examination and inspection of your relationship and help each of you to add your own personal conditions, contingencies and points of view and to inspect the overall attitude of your relationship.

Above all, be compassionate, gentle and a friend to your lover or husband.

BEGINNINGS

What attracted you to your spouse/lover when you first met?

What were your hopes and expectations when you decided to make a commitment to this person?

What is your image of the ideal relationship?

What three things do you find most stressful about your spouse or lover or the relationship?

How do you usually cope with these stresses?

How successful are you in coping?

If you found someone else with whom you could be intimate both sexually and emotionally, would you leave your spouse/lover?

GENERAL RELATIONSHIP QUESTIONS

What about morals and ethics? Do you or your spouse/lover share morals and ethics? If so, name the most important. If not, explain.

Do you and your spouse/lover have mutual goals? Do you want them?

Do you feel that someone must fulfill your needs, or are you independent?

What are your most significant needs? Affection, attention, approval, reassurance, praise? If not these, what are your needs?

Does your spouse/lover fulfill these needs? Do you want him to fulfill these needs?

Do you need to be intellectually stimulated and have your mind challenged? In what ways?

How often do you laugh? What do you laugh at?

Do you laugh at the same things that your spouse/lover laughs at?

Do you have fun together?

Are you friends?

Is your spouse/lover your best friend? What does "best friend" mean to you?

How much patience do you have?

If your spouse/lover lacks patience, can you live with this?

Can you live with your spouse/lover's shortcomings? Some might include impatience, drinking, too much golf, and too much work.

Do you or your spouse/lover take risks i.e., bungee jumping, risky financial investments, reckless driving? Would you consider this a shortcoming? Why or why not?

In what ways would you believe an extra-marital affair is a risk?

Do you believe your spouse/lover has a strong ego? Would you consider this a shortcoming? Why or why not?

When you are dissatisfied, do you blame yourself or your spouse/lover?

Do you feel that you are duty-bound to _____ or to be _____ because of the marriage contract? i.e., not lie, faithful, etc.

Do you expect your spouse/lover to take care of you and be the stronger personality?

Are you dependent on your spouse/lover?

Do you want to be the dominant partner? In what ways?

Do you attend to your personal appearance for your spouse/lover?

Are you observant of your spouse/lover? In what ways?

Do you feel loved and understood by your spouse/lover? How does he show his love?

Do you feel respected by him? Do you respect him?

Do you approve and accept him? Does he approve and accept you?

Are you protective of him? In what ways?

COMMUNICATION

Do you feel as if you communicate well with your spouse/lover?

Do you trust your spouse/lover?

Do you share your deepest and most intimate thoughts and secrets with your spouse/lover?

Do you make eye contact with your spouse/lover?

Do you give demanding orders? Do you find this acceptable?

Do you allow your spouse/lover to tell you what to do even though you resent it?

Do you speak to your spouse/lover with terms of endearment? (honey, love)

How varied are your topics of conversation? What do you talk about?

Do you ask many questions?

How well do you explain things?

Are you detailed with your messages?

Do you feel your spouse/lover listens to you?

Do you praise your spouse/lover? In what ways?

Do you interrupt your spouse/lover when you are talking? If so, when does this happen?

How is your voice when you speak? Does it annoy your spouse/lover?

Do you encourage your spouse/lover?

Do you nag or blame?

How are your conversation skills?

Can you ask your spouse/lover for help?

Are you afraid to disagree or argue with your spouse/lover?

Are you aggressive?

Do you smile when you see your spouse/lover?

How do you fight? Do you insult people when you fight? i.e., spouse/lover, in-laws, siblings etc.

During a dispute, do you stick to the subject or bring other past "sins" into the scenario?

Do you say, "I'm sorry," after a dispute or if you hurt someone?

Do you seek sympathy from your spouse/lover?

Do you talk on the phone constantly, during meals, in car, in bed?

Do you feel distant from your spouse/lover? Describe the distance you feel.

SEX

Compatibility with another person goes beyond the sex act itself. Human sexuality brings along with it cultures, rituals, and mores as well as morals. Unlike animals where instincts prevail, humans give boundaries to sex. Humans have the capacity to be attracted to another person who will fulfill a value and meaning from the attracted person.

Barry L. Duncan, Psy.D, and Joseph W. Rock, Psy.D, say it best in their book, *Overcoming Relationship Impasses: Ways to Initiate Change When Your Partner Won't Help*, "Key aspects of couples' sex lives have little to do with what happens in bed. Quality and quantity of communication, mutual respect and feelings of emotional safety and trust have much more of an impact on most people's levels of sexual intimacy than do the partners' technical proficiency or choices of cologne."

How open are you with your spouse/lover about your sexual needs?

Are you satisfied with your sex?

Do you make love often enough for you? For him?

Do you really know what makes your spouse/lover have an orgasm?

Do you talk when you are making love?

Do you say what your spouse/lover wants to hear?

Do you know what your spouse/lover wants to hear?

Do you practice foreplay?

What do you want to see during sex? Do you want to be exposed to erotic movies, pictures or stories?

Do you have to be in control of the lovemaking? Do you feel uncomfortable if you are not in control?

Who should initiate sex?

Do you feel desirable to your spouse/lover?

Do you hold each other and kiss hello/goodbye?

Do you want to be complimented during sex? i.e., Your spouse/lover likes your breasts.

Do you know your spouse/lover's romantic fantasies?

Do you know where your spouse/lover wants to be touched?

Do you like oral sex?

Where is your favorite place to make love?

Where on the body do you like to be kissed?

Are you aware of when your spouse/lover wants to make love or does not want to make love?

YOUR HOME

If you divorce your husband, where will you live? Will you keep your home?

Do you feel comfortable in your home?

Do you both agree on what your home will look like?

Do you have your own personal space in your home?

Do you both agree on where your home should be located?

Who is/will be responsible for what chores?

What kind of bed do/will you have?

How much will you spend on your home?

Who will decide on the decorations?

Will any family live with you?

MONEY

If you divorce or remarry, or if you are marrying for the first time, will you have a prenuptial agreement?

If you divorce your spouse, how will you support yourself?

If either of you have children, will you have to provide a home for them?

Will your finances be kept separate from your new mate? How will you determine when and if you will have joint financial accounts?

How much money do you make as a couple?

Together do you make enough to satisfy your needs and expenses?

Together what are your expenses? How important is a budget to your overall financial health?

Do you have financial goals?

Do you want to keep set amounts in your checking and savings accounts?

What percentage of your earnings will you invest? What will you invest in?

Will it be necessary to decide jointly on purchases? Over $100? Over $50? Over $25?

Will you have joint or individual accounts?

Who will be responsible for paying the bills?

What about insurance? Health, life, homeowners, car?

Do you support any charity? Do you pay tithes or fees to a church or synagogue, or dues to a club or other group?

Does your spouse/lover gamble? Do you approve?

WORK

Are you both content with your jobs?

Are your hours of work clearly defined? Time at home?

How involved in each other's work should you become?
When do you want to retire?

HEALTH

How do you feel about physical exercise? Is it important to a successful marriage?

How does your spouse/lover feel about eating and meals? Who will shop, cook and clean up?

Do you know what foods your spouse/lover enjoys?

Do you have any concerns about exercising, weight control, high cholesterol, high blood pressure?

What about drinking? Do you approve or disapprove of heavy drinking? Moderate drinking? Social drinking?

Is alcoholism a factor in your marriage or relationship?

Is your spouse/lover in need of extra care physically? If so, does this extra care pose a financial problem?

How do you feel about how your spouse/lover addresses health concerns?

What about smoking? Can you tolerate smoking? Do you smoke? What about him?

Do you feel your spouse/lover could be healthier? Are you concerned about any health issues?

Does your spouse/lover have emotional problems that warrant medical treatment?

Is your spouse/lover a hypochondriac?

How do you feel about farting, snoring and burping that are not symptoms of a serious ailment? Are they non-issues?

FAMILY

Do you have family customs and/or rituals that may interfere or enhance your relationship?

Does your spouse/lover have family customs and/or rituals that may interfere or enhance your relationship?

Do you both celebrate the same holidays? If not, does this create problems?

Where will you spend the holidays?

What about visiting the relatives for birthdays, anniversaries and celebrations?

Will you have a pre-set budget for gifts?

How does you spouse/lover feel about your relationship with your family?

How do you feel about his relationship with his family?

Are you close to your brothers and sisters? Is he with his?

Is your spouse/lover relaxed with your family? Are you with his?

Are there any boundaries about spending time with each other's families?

Do you visit your families often? Too often? Not often enough?

CHILDREN

Do either of you have children?

If not, do you want to have children? How many? When?

If you find that you are physically unable to have children, will you consider adoption?

Have you set limits on how much time your children will spend with each other's families?

Do you expect your children to be close to their grandparents and/or aunts and uncles?

Will one of you stay home while the children are growing up?

Will it be necessary to have outside help such as nanny, or housekeeper, or to use a service such as a day care center?

In what faith will your children be raised: Jewish, Protestant, Roman Catholic, Muslim, Buddhist, Hindu, or other?

Will you raise your children as atheists?

What about children from previous marriages/relationships?

What are your expectations regarding discipline and education?

How much time will you spend with the children?

Will each child have a separate room?

THE SOCIAL SCENE

Are outside friendships important to your relationship?

How often do you socialize?

Do you socialize too much? Too little?

Are you secure with your spouse/lover's friends? Is he with yours?

Do you have mutual friends?

Does your spouse/lover object to your friends of the opposite sex?

What about hobbies, sports, and recreation ? Tennis? Golf? Yoga? Internet?

RELIGION

Do you both have the same religion?

Where do religion and spirituality fit into your lives?

If your spouse/lover doesn't practice any religion nor have an interest in spirituality, will he object to your spending time in worship? Can he respect your choice?

How much time do you expect to devote to your religion every week?

LETTING GO (Some couples will not need this section.)

Do you want your relationship to end?

Do you feel that you settled for less of a person than you deserve with your spouse/lover?

Do you feel you have to end your marriage to preserve your sanity? Explain

Do you believe that ending your marriage is best for yourself and your children?

Do you feel confident that you can make it alone? Are you afraid of being alone?

Are you willing to give up the security blanket of your home?

Are you afraid of change? The future? Risk-taking?

Are you unsure of yourself?

Do you anticipate the best or the worst?

Are you willing to give up the social status that marriage confers?

Do you believe that an unhappy marriage can be far more destructive than a divorce for children?

Do you believe that children from divorced homes are better adjusted than children from intact, unhappy homes?

CHAPTER TWELVE

Statistics and Facts

"Smoking is one of the leading causes of statistics."
Fletcher Knebel

"Statistics show that of those who contract the habit of eating, very few survive."
Wallace Irwin

"There are three kinds of lies: lies, damned lies, and statistics."
Disraeli

DESENSITIZATION

In recent years, with the prevalence of many widely publicized scandalous affairs, the media and violent shifts in ethics has desensitized the words "adultery" and "affairs," along with the sanctity and virtue of the marriage vows. Most everyone is confused regarding the morally right or wrong thing to do. Just as children today are desensitized regarding violence from various media sources, violence and adultery seem to be the subject matter that widely predominate everyone's everyday life. The Clinton White House fiasco is an example of how moral and ethical standards are changing. Many people's position regarding adultery has been that what you do behind closed doors is your business; it doesn't necessarily effect your performance regarding your career or reflect your character. This excerpt from the book *Uncoupling: The Art of Coming Apart: A Guide to Sane Divorce,* by Norman Sheresky and Marya Mannes, sums up the general feeling regarding adultery today:

"Thou shalt not kill. Thou shalt not steal. Thou shalt not covet thy neighbor's wife (nor her ass). Thou shalt not commit adultery. In our present climate, killing is an hourly fact, stealing a political act (coveting and taking are synonymous), and adultery is considered by many to be as archaic as the sanctity it violates. What comes naturally is natural for the natural man. To him (or her) guilt is a hang-up, self-control a drag, indulgence a civil right. The righteous may still thunder from pulpits, and God-fearing citizens compress their lips in abhorrence, but even the law is now powerless to restrain the open expression of man's instinctual nature. Long legal and religious suppression, in fact, of its healthier manifestations bears considerable responsibility for the explosion of its sicker ones. And among the healthier manifestations now recognized by students of man is the open acceptance of sex, not only within but outside of marriage, as an essential human expression as well as need."

This controversial stance is a subliminal image or glimpse that represents the subconscious opinions of people today regarding adultery. We must remember, however, that humans give boundaries to their sexual instincts and attach rituals and culture to compatibility with one another for a deep relationship experience to fulfill their purpose and significance. Yes, standards regarding adultery, sex and affairs are changing but humans must remain more responsible in their quest for self-fulfillment.

STATISTICS AND PERCENTAGES

The validity of statistics regarding sexuality is difficult to determine or establish because it is complicated. The results of categorizing the contrasting standards of morality or proving and documenting different patterns of sexual behavior across religions, cultures and societies to create a standard or consensus regarding sexuality prove to be inconsistent. However, pinpointing what people think about sex and how different people view sexual pleasure or commitment and under what conditions, can enable our society to understand if change is taking place. Once it is established that change in sexual attitudes is happening, we can better comprehend and sense how this change will effect our lives. These changes in our society, such as divorce and extra-marital affairs, effect our children and the future of our society, as we know it. They also serve to give all of us a glimpse into the fabric of our social lives and provide a mirror for us to view how we conduct ourselves as humans. Fortunately, there have been many major studies investigating sexual attitude and behavior. Unfortunately, the methods and conditions under which these surveys have been taken remain questionable.

Educational levels, financial status, religion and whether or not people feel comfortable or free from embarrassment and self-consciousness are factors that must be considered when attempting to accumulate facts about sexuality that can lead to generalizing a particular society's sexual preferences, attitudes and behaviors. Survey takers must determine if these factors and characteristics are considered, and then reflected, in patterns of sexual behavior. Additionally, questions arise as to whether the information gathered was in fact a survey or an observational study. Also, one must ask if the sexual behavior and attitudes of women and men were taken into consideration, since women and men have different understandings and different behavioral practices regarding sex and what's more the truthfulness of the people who participate in the survey is important.

When we look at statistics, we tend to measure ourselves with the survey results. In turn we might find ourselves wondering if we have missed something important in our lives and therefore find ourselves wanting. Thereby we persuade ourselves into acceptance with what we perceive to be the accepted norm in sexual behavior.

How can anyone accurately elicit personal sensitive information from total strangers for public scrutiny? Who would want to relive the painful episodes of their lives if they have labored to come to an amicable peace with their spouse and answer any survey asking if they had ever participated in an extra-marital affair? Or for that matter, who, if they are having an affair, a term which implies confidence and secrecy, will admit to their secret tryst simply to satisfy a poll seeking to gather information for the general public or for any study?

According to Janet Reibstein, Ph.D and Martin Richards, Ph.D, in their book, *Sexual Arrangements: Marriage and the Temptation of Infidelity*, "People do not want to admit to affairs because they clearly do not approve of their own behavior. More than that, if they acknowledge their affairs, they might be discovered, and if discovered, their marriages could be wrecked. So most studies have had to make do with the samples of people they could recruit either through press advertisements or through something called the "snowball" method (interview one person and get him or her to suggest another person to be interviewed) or through clinical samples, such as people in marital therapy. These are not representative samples; they do not accurately reflect the population at large, since they have been self-selected or selected in other biased ways. Any conclusions drawn from them are therefore shaky and will not necessarily hold for the population at large."

On the other hand, research indicates that those who have experienced an affair are suffering personally and are somewhat relieved when they discuss their trials and tribulations. As a result, the statistics regarding people who have had an affair or who are thinking about an affair or who are currently engaged in an affair range from eighty-five percent to thirty percent accuracy. The statistics are conflicting and they fluctuate drastically depending on the sex of the respondents or other factors.

Comprehensive statistics representing a summary of non-scientific surveys reveal that approximately seventy percent of all married men and fifty percent of all married women have affairs, and one partner will have an affair in approximately eighty percent of all marriages. About sixty percent of all single men and women have had an intimate relationship with a married person. The percentages of affairs in trusted and committed unmarried couples are even higher.

According to the United States Census Bureau, Statistical Abstract of the United States 1999 edition...

The total number of marriages in the United States in 1997 was 2,383,700.

The total number of divorces was 870,600.

For women ages fifteen to forty-four of all races, a 1988 survey monitoring first-marriage dissolution and years until remarriage for separation and divorce reveals that although affairs are common, people generally do not talk about them.

The total number of male sexual partners in a lifetime for women surveyed by the National Center for Health Statistics, based on interviews conducted in person in homes of 10,847 women ages fifteen to forty-four were: zero partners 10.5%, one partner 23.5%, two partners 12.3%, three partners 9.6%, four partners 8.4%, five partners 8.1%, six to nine partners 12.1%, ten or more partners 15.5%.

The total number of unmarried couples under twenty-five to over seventy-five years old in 1998, defined as two unrelated adults of the opposite sex sharing the same household, was 4,236,000.

The total number of married couples in 1998 fifteen to seventy-five years of age was 55,305,000.

FACTS

As mentioned earlier, this book is a compendium of research and psychologists' points of view. The facts gathered here are a summary of views compiled over a four-year period.

Affairs occur because of needs such as emotional satisfaction more than sexual gratification and physical attraction.

People engage in affairs because they are healing and are good for personal growth.

Not all affairs end in divorce; and forty-five percent of those engaged in an affair admit it to their spouse.

Religion does not become a factor in affairs. Those people who have affairs ignore their religious affiliations that discourage their affairs.

Some affairs last a lifetime.

According to Lana Staheli, Ph.d. in her book *Triangles: Understanding, Preventing, and Surviving an Affair*:

Fewer than 10% of people in affairs divorce their spouse then marry their lover.

Nearly eighty percent of those who divorce because of an affair are sorry later.

Over seventy-five percent of affair-marriages end in divorce.

For those whose marriages survive affairs, recovery takes between one and three years.

Getting rid of the spouse does not get rid of the pain.

Healing from a divorce takes about three years, children pay a high price, and many spouses remain bitter for decades.

Most marriages survive an affair. If you want to stay married, you can.

CHAPTER THIRTEEN

Contradictions

"I only like two kinds of men: domestic and foreign."
Mae West

"By the time we've made it, we've had it."
Malcolm Forbes

"Hope is the feeling you have that the feeling you have isn't permanent."
Jean Kerr

"If this is coffee, please bring me some tea; but if this is tea, please bring me some coffee."
Abraham Lincoln

BEYOND STEREOTYPE AND MORALITY

So far no one has any definitive, viable answers regarding the reason, reasons or lack of reasoning as to why anyone would have an extra-marital affair. Despite the warnings, risks and all the evidence that is presented against having extra-marital affairs, they are still very common. The statistics are overwhelming. Why?

We can only guess and ask significant questions to gain knowledge into the reasons for extra-marital affairs. Experts have been baffled, giving many theories and educated observations. In the course of extensive research, those people who try to explain this phenomenon only succumb to society's rules and regulations regarding moral and righteous actions. The experts' explanations center on need fulfillment and the sickness of the initiator of an affair. Their conclusions implicate the morally right or wrong thing to do.

Taboos always attract us, for better or for worse. Acting and behaving ninety-five percent of the time according to society's rules and cultural stereotyping and acting in your own best interest behind closed doors five percent of the time gives many people a certain fulfillment and inner joy that nothing else can allow. For example, why do women want to be seduced? The appeal of a man who is not her husband and who steps outside of the stereotypical norms of good mystifies and elicits a desire so strong that she acts to fulfill a need long suppressed. She has satisfied the needs of her spouse and children and seeks satisfaction for herself through an extra-marital affair. She can connect with this "other" man on a visceral level and court him, as she wants to be courted. This power becomes a compulsion to free herself on a sensual plane and it is this power that could cost her everything and at the same time present her with opportunities to explore and accomplish an inner satisfaction that cannot be satiated by any other means. Emotional seduction becomes a very powerful element in her decision to go beyond her wedding vows and seek that one ingredient that cannot be satisfied through the commonplace requirements for self-satisfaction.

What is going on in this scenario? This woman cannot be labeled an adulteress or immoral. She is not self-centered. She is in touch with her inner need to balance her responsibilities and at the same time respond to her own highest good. This adds to her self-image and helps her to feel and confirm her real self. It is her strength and it is also, according to many, her ultimate demise because self-centeredness is not generally accepted.

She has her earnest and respectful husband and has established herself as a God-fearing upstanding citizen, but this power to fulfill a desire, which is labeled taboo, causes her to go beyond and seek personal gratification.

A philosophy that has been adopted in recent times is that you should never neglect your own basic needs and that each individual's well-being should be satisfied before the individual's family or spouse. Maintaining a satisfactory emotional balance for yourself will only serve the greater need of your family if you are first content. When you are content you become a better person. Contentment breeds success.

This philosophy compels us to continually ask ourselves what is right or wrong, and in the process we become detached from feeling for others who are important to us. Indifference becomes a justification for taking care of our own needs. We embrace this attitude in our own private life by satisfying our emotional balance that right and wrong, which are dictates from society on the outside, do not come into play. Indifference and self-fulfillment come from within the person's aspirations and the person's idea of what is good for that person.

Another philosophy is the NO rationale. N = Neglect and O = Omission. We do not neglect society's rules or omit our responsibilities, but maintain our emotional sanity through an affair, which allows us to not neglect or omit our own personal needs. It is a catch twenty-two situation. Under this concept, any attempt at an affair does not work and is contradictory. For example, if an affair makes you neglect your children, your responsibilities have been omitted and the affair becomes disadvantageous. The question is then, "What purpose does this affair serve?" Does it maintain our emotional sanity by not neglecting or omitting our own personal needs? You are still suffering in order to satisfy your emotional and personal needs and you become frustrated and repressed because in your own mind, you must satisfy the needs of your family first.

According to the NO theory, an affair makes you frustrated and gives you cause to act out in a negative way, such as taking less time with your children or being irritable because you cannot be with your lover. As a result the affair is operating at the expense of your responsibilities and you are paying the consequences of your actions. This affair does not enhance your well-being but instead damages your inner peace because it makes your life chaotic.

TABOOS

Extra-marital sex arises from a desire to serve and satisfy innate desires and needs. However, it is a contradiction because basic Judeo-Christian values make it a taboo to address the self. Although it is a natural tendency to follow our desires, at the same time it is a dilemma because right and wrong do not come into play in the mind of the person committing adultery or engaging in an extra-marital affair. However, the questions "What must you be compelled to do?" and "What must you be compelled not to do?" challenge the people involved in an affair constantly. Distressingly, there are never any answers, only contradictions and it is usually the circumstances that dictate decisions. Circumstances dictate choice and eventually the consequences of that choice.

One might argue that it is basic human nature to take care of us first and protect our emotional balance above all else. How we should conduct ourselves in our daily activities generally reflects our character and our goodness. Yet with extra-marital affairs, the participants contradict these morally correct actions. Promises to be faithful till death involve remaining faithful. This is an unbending rule that challenges many couples.

Many people have challenged this notion and question who is to judge what is right and what is wrong. It is argued that it is up to each individual to determine what is right and wrong and what the truth of a situation is.

One could reason to oneself that it is never right to cheat on your spouse because it is a breach of trust and your promise to remain faithful. But when confronted with the desire to fill a void and have an extra-marital affair, something can take over, desire, making you contradict everything you believed was reasonable.

Many people argue that self-control and commitment must regulate and govern our decisions regarding our marriage contract. Even those who decide to have an extra-marital affair often believe they are committed to their spouse but contradict themselves with their actions. All this in the name of self-preservation.

Love, self-control, commitment, sacrifice and family are all good moral reasons to be faithful to your spouse, but there are countless examples throughout history where the contradictions glare at us. Having their cake and eating it too, many have indulged while at the same time remained married. Principles and morality by today's Western standards are checked at the hotel desk during an affair. While some people believe that a person having an extra-marital affair has a weak spirit, a growing number of people applaud them as pioneers who seek self-preservation and fulfillment.

Put yourself on the other side of the fence: How would you feel if your spouse were to do this to you?

Getting yourself caught up in a guilty situation, and believing you are wrong and buying into the harsh reality that your actions are despicable will lead you down the road to self-degradation or repentance and reform. If, however, you do not see your actions as wrong but as vehicles to personal happiness and self-fulfillment, your actions represent beliefs, a value that you believe is right. Perhaps you believe that this value you have espoused (to engage in extra-marital sex is okay) is a value that society has

accepted without question and demands moral justification for your actions, which you are not about to embrace.
Yet, when you marched down the aisle you followed all of
your society's cultural traditions and mandates and married into a specific value system. Contradiction?

Perhaps, then, you believe that what is good and bad,
right or wrong, must rely completely on the convictions of
people: If one takes away everyone's beliefs about right
and wrong, good and bad, then right and wrong, and good
and bad go away. In effect, you believe that it is okay to
have an extra-marital affair because you believe that it is
the belief of everyone else. It is what you believe is right,
and this makes it right. What happens if you change your
mind? Will having an extra-marital affair then be wrong
because you and everyone else now believe that it is wrong?

This is an example of a moral dilemma where you find
yourself in a situation in which, apparently, the right or
proper thing to do seems to conflict with the course of action you think would benefit you the most or make you the
happiest. You take the course of action that you believe
will be the one most likely to guide you to your own well-
being. You are not swayed by the idea that temperance and
restraint influence goodness. In your quest for happiness
and concern for your own welfare, do you compromise your
regard for what is considered the "common good" or your
family's needs, or society's dictates?

Many people today in our society subscribe to a go-for-it
philosophy. They believe that life should be dedicated to
the acquisition of many pleasures. This is an age-old concept called hedonism and it has evidently resurfaced with
today's open sexuality. They believe that a life without pleasure is ambiguous and boring. They also believe that a life
without pain is just as boring. Again, we must ask ourselves,
if we follow this principle, would we compromise the greater
good of those who are most significant in our lives for our
own self-interest.

But in the matter of the preservation of their own lives, people who seek personal survival above all things and direct all of their energy toward this end find that they become somewhat limited. They promise to uphold laws and contracts that keep them from indulging in personal pleasure to satisfy their own needs and desires at the expense of others' liberties.

Think further about this concept. When we act to please our moral consciousness, we identify with a generous character or personality. When we are approved for this morally conscious act, it is our character that is approved and not our actions. By living within your marriage contract and keeping your promise to remain faithful, you are acting as a morally conscious adult.

The contradiction comes when we believe that by having an extra-marital affair to satisfy our own self-interest we do not break any rules, that rules are set forth by our society, that, in the moral sense, we consider to be bad, wrong, unjust and contemptible; if we believe that ultimate happiness is found in the preservation of our own personal needs and wants. Again, the contradiction comes between what is good for us and what we must be compelled to do out of the concern for others.

Many people get simple pleasure by caring for others and believe that this is important to their own self-interest. They believe that they can care for another person and at the same time look out for themselves. This is one principle that a loving marriage is built upon, and it is a principle that carries many people through a tough decision to decide not to cheat on their spouse.

WHY YOU SHOULD DO WHAT YOU SHOULD DO

There are essential moral and ethical dictates to which our society holds our behavior without exception. Murder and stealing from one another are prime examples. However, extra-marital sex is a gray area. These are legal rules that command obedience for the sake of no other end other than the rule's own rightness. Western society maintains that you should remain loyal and faithful to your spouse because it is the right thing to do and you promised to do so.

For example, when you marry, you promise to remain faithful forever. What about when you break your promise and indulge in extra-marital sex for the sake of your own happiness and your own welfare? You are not foregoing your moral duty to remain faithful because it is simply your moral duty. You are foregoing your promise because it serves your own self-preservation and happiness.

Your intention to break your promise means that you have given considerable thought to your actions, are in control of your own decisions, and therefore will be responsible for all of the consequences. Calculating the extent of the consequences enables you to consider the probable consequences before you act, with particular regard to how many people your decision will effect. How much pleasure is worth any pain or consequences that will result over the long run? Finally, when you give higher priority to your own happiness above others, you are forever grappling with a basic decision, which is self over others. Again, by seeking a full measure of pleasure for yourself you are compromising everyone else's considerations.

The quality of the pleasure you seek in an affair can be measured when you consider what happens on the downside of an affair that becomes ugly because of hidden agendas, revenge, immaturity, blind rebellion, senselessness and stupidity. Affairs may have different implications, such as, a hidden agenda, which involves revenge against a spousal conflict or misunderstanding. It is also a senseless move whereby two people seek each other's comfort, because a bad situation doesn't change by a senseless move. An affair could also be pathetic, part of an expression of immaturity, in which an individual seeks to escape from a no-exit situation of a relationship. It could be blind rebellion against societal dictates, regardless of long-term consequences such as energy spent in self-preservation rather than self-progression, or sexually transmitted diseases.

The question remains "What makes a great percentage of people have affairs?" This question cannot be answered with simple, absolute explanations because of the many contradictions and different situations and points of view involved in the complexities of human interaction.

When confronted with making a disconcerting or troubling decision, we have, first of all, an obligation to think about it and to examine all of the options available to us. After we review the situation, we will realize that nothing is ever set in stone and these decisions will always produce a new situation, with its own new dilemmas, forcing us to take on other challenges. Nothing is ever decided once and for all. Situations change, and the more flexible our decision, the better suited it is to the messy world of human conduct.

Acting responsibly and not on impulse obliges us to commit ourselves to reason and rationality. It is important to take into consideration all people who have a risk in the outcome of our decision and look at all options from this detached point of view. This involves giving equal consideration to the rights, interests, and choices of all of the people whom your decision will effect. In other words, will everyone be counted in the decision? Ask yourself how you would feel if someone did this to you. It is impossible to be totally conscientious and credible if we do not take these points into consideration.

On the other hand, many people believe in biased and individual or personal choices that are influenced by what something or someone else dictates. Such dictates include customs, cultures or simply their own desires. In other words, each person has the right to decide on all matters of right and wrong. What is right for you may not be right for me and vise versa, and no one has any right to impose one's morality on anyone else. This is justified by our fundamental belief and protected by Freedom of Speech. This permits each person (within certain limits) to express his or her opinion without interference.

Furthermore, we live in a society where many different cultures co-exist. We agree that the instinctive inborn honor of each individual is to maintain his or her own identity, including different beliefs and teachings. We have a duty to treat all people with respect and accept them and the culture from which they come.

The most important point of all of this choice is that the theory of relative ethics, which we have been discussing, is flawed because what you have a right to do and the right thing to do cannot be connected logically. You have the right to contradict yourself and believe that one and one is five but that does not make your choice correct. No one has any right to impose his values on anyone else. Respect for the individual and for individual liberty, along with cultural diversity, are values that you are probably perfectly content to accept as almost absolute and certainly permanent. One would agree on the soundness of this argument. But, according to this line of reasoning, I have no right to object to your attempts or the Moral Majority's, or Hitler's, to impose values on me. According to relative ethics, if imposing values is one of the things you like to do, just because it really feels good to impose values, then it's obviously right, for you, to impose values on me and I have no grounds for protest.

Once you have asserted that no one has the right to correct you when you express your opinions, you certainly seem to have told me that any such opinions are right, or at least as right as opinions can be. Without argument, the integrity of every human thought, the sanctity of individual rights, the autonomy and dignity of the person, the appreciation of cultural variety are all real human values worthy of positive feedback.

Consider the no-resolution problem of abortion. One side is bound by religious and moral obligations to speak up and protest against the "slaughter of the unborn." They cite moral rules and rights—Natural Law, the Ten Commandments, the Right to Life, which hold regardless of situation or consequence. However, the other side calls attention to the pain felt by the women contemplating unwanted pregnancy, the deaths of women prior to *Roe vs. Wade*, the negative effects on employment, education costs and other negative outcomes that arise from denying abortions. One side focuses on the nature of the abortion act itself and the other side focuses on problems they are solving by allowing abortion. They can never come to resolution because they refuse to countenance the other side's position. When both sides can acknowledge that each other's point of view is justifiable and warranted, even while knowing that they can never convert the other side, then they have a possibility of coming to an alternative workable solution and living along side each other. When there is no possibility of agreeing with the other's moral stand, there is no hope of destroying the other. In other words, neither one is going away. Each must learn to live with the other in peace, even while retaining the conviction that what the other is doing is fundamentally wrong, immoral or mistaken.

CONCLUSION

Sex is a natural human tendency. Religions, cultures, and societies of our world, which attach and dictate rules and regulations for this natural human tendency, are practicing a gross interference. Those who go outside of their respective religions, cultures or societies suffer consequences to the extent of being labeled social deviates. By this very fact of creating taboos within the family and marriage institution, affairs receive a moral standard, which is an unnecessary strain on individual well-being, because no one wants to be deviate.

The difference between keeping a promise because that is what society dictates is right or keeping a promise out of fear of the consequences is what precipitates change in the over all morality of a generation. It is an age-old dilemma that is not an original thought and this author cannot claim credit. Should we keep our promises because it is our duty to do so and because we know from basic knowledge that keeping promises is right and good? Should we live in the way that society tells us is ideal? Or should we keep our promises because we are afraid of the consequences if we do not? Should we follow our ego and our own self-interest or should we follow what is beneficial for the welfare of others?

Does your action make sense and can you rationalize it and justify it? Who is to say what reason is the correct reason when you take into consideration all of the circumstances involved in each person's individual circumstances?

If you make a moral claim that extramarital sex is wrong or that extra-marital sex must be justified, can it be defended and supported by an argument that will be reasonable for all parties involved?

Is the virtue of temperance or self-control over your physical desires a morally excellent virtue that enables any person to be happy? Can restraint be characterized as a virtue that works for your own well-being and not get you into trouble? Would you say that people who engage in extra-marital sex simply don't know any better and are ignorant of good moral behavior and are misdirected or are they not in love with their spouse?

Contrarily, is that person who engages in extra-marital sex taking action because of pure emotion because they are suffering due to a lack of something, i.e. attention?

Would you assume that it is right to not betray your spouse because of duty and respect and because it is the principal of the situation to simply keep your promise and that consequences are irrelevant to your reasoning?

Or is the rightness of your action juxtaposed with the happiness it produces as its consequence? You have an extra-marital affair because it makes you happy, fulfills a basic need and as a result of your happiness everyone in your family is happy. Therefore, your actions produced the greatest amount of happiness for all involved and the consequences resulted in good.

Morality, then, is a set of rules that is best for everyone in a particular society that serves the interests of the majority of the people in that society. Morality is not what is best for an individual but is a set of rules governed by God, by society, a group, or by reason. Our society dictates that it is morally wrong to have an extra-marital affair and that when you go beyond your wedding vows that you promised to death do you part to remain faithful to your spouse you are morally wrong. The question that this book has attempted to answer is "Is our society changing its moral standard?" Given all of the evidence presented thus far and the overwhelming statistics that suggest that many people are engaging in extra-marital sex, it is evident that the standards regarding taboos and extra-marital sex and monogamy are changing. But how we respond to this phenomenon, and how we effect society, or how we allow it to affect us, is an individual choice. Don't become a victim to this choice, take responsibility for yourself.

Bibliography

Only When I Laugh A Post-Marriage Adventure—Hazardous, Hilarious, and True, Erica Abeel. W. Morrow, New York, 1978.

Inside Divorce—Is It What You Really Want?, Edmond Addeo and Robert Burger. Chilton Book Company, Radnor, PA, 1975.

Life After Divorce Love In An Age of Divorce, A. Alvarez. Simon and Schuster a Division of Gulf and Western Corporation, New York, 1981.

Divorce and the American Family, Jan Andrew. F. Watts, New York, 1978.

This Wasn't Supposed to Happen: Single Women Over Thirty Talk Frankly About Their Lives, Susan Crain Bakos. Continuum, New York, 1985.

Sudden Endings: Wife Rejection in Happy Marriages, Madeline Bennett. Morrow, New York, 1991 .

The Other Man, The Other Woman: Understanding and Coping with Extramarital Affairs, Joel D. Block, Ph.D. Grosset & Dunlap, New York, 1978.

Family—The Ties That Bind...and Gag!, Erma Bombeck. McGraw-Hill Book Company, New York, 1987.

Lethal Lovers and Poisonous People: How to Protect Your Health From Relationships That Make You Sick, Harriet B. Braiker, Ph.D. Pocket Books, New York, 1992.

But I Didn't Want A Divorce Putting Your Life Back Together, André Bustanoby. Zondervan, Grand Rapids, 1978.

1,911 Best Things Anybody Ever Said, Robert Byrne. Fawcett Columbine, Published by Ballantine Books, New York, 1988.

Marriage Divorce Remarriage, Andrew J. Cherlin. Harvard University Press, Cambridge, Massachusetts, 1981.

Smart Women Foolish Choices: Finding the Right Man and Avoiding the Wrong Ones, Dr. Connell Cowan and Dr. Melvyn Kinder. Clarkson N. Potter, Inc., Crown Publishers, New York, 1985.

Love Me, Love Me Not: How to Survive Infidelity, Daniel J. Dolesh and Sherelynn Lehman. McGraw-Hill, New York, 1985.

Overcoming Relationship Impasses: Ways to Initiate Change When Your Partner Won't Help, Barry L. Duncan Psy.D. and Joseph W. Rock, Psy.D. Insight Books, New York, 1991.

Divorced In America Marriage; In An Age of Possibility, Joseph Epstein. Dutton, New York, 1974.

Woman Versus Woman: The Extramarital Affair, Shirley Eskapa. F. Watts, New York, 1984.

Rebuilding—When Your Relationship Ends, Bruce Fisher. Impact Publishers, San Luis Obispo, California, 1985.

Anatomy of Love: The Natural History of Monogamy, Adultery, and Divorce, Helen E. Fisher, Ph.D. WW Norton and Company, New York, London, 1992.

His Affair: The Powerful True Story of One Woman's Confrontation With Every Woman's Nightmare, Jo Fleming. M. Evans and Company, Philadelphia, 1976.

How Can I Get Through To You? Breakthrough Communication—Beyond Gender, Beyond Therapy, Beyond Deception, D. Glenn Foster and Mary Marshall..Hyperion, New York, 1994.

Secret Loves Women With Two Lives, Sonya Friedman, Ph.D. Crown Publishers, Inc., New York, 1994.

The Psychologist Looks At Sex and Marriage, Allan Fromme. Prentice-Hall, Inc., New York, 1950.

Extraordinary Relationships: A New Way of Thinking About Human Interactions, Roberta Gilbert. M.D. John Wiley & Sons, Inc., New York, Chichester, 1992.

He Says, She says: Closing the Communication Gap Between the Sexes, Lillian Glass, Ph.D. G.P. Putnam's Sons, New York, 1992.

Marriage, Love, Sex and Divorce What Brings Us Together, What Drives Us Apart, Jonathan Gathorne-Hardy. Summit Books, A Simon & Schuster Division of Gulf and Western Corporation, New York, 1981.

The Erotic Silence of the American Wife, Delma Heyn. Turtle Bay Books, Division of Random House, New York, 1992.

Smart Women, Smart Choices: Set Limits and Gain Control of Your Personal and Professional Life, Hattie Hill. Golden Books, New York, 1998.

The Affair: A Portrait of Extra-Marital Love in Contemporary America, Morton Hunt.

An NAL Book. The World Publishing Company, New York, Cleveland, 1969.

The Mistress, Wendy James and Susan Jane Kedgley. Abelard-Schuman, London, 1973.

Women on Divorce A Bedside Companion, edited By Penny Kaganoff and Susan Spano. Harcourt Brace & Co., New York, 1995.

The Dynamics of Divorce; A Life Cycle Perspective, Florence W. Kaslow and Lita Linzer Schwartz. Brunner/Mazel, New York, 1987.

Learning to Love Again, Mel Krantzler. Harper and Row, New York, 1977.

Affair Prevention: Specific Techniques That Can Strengthen and Protect Your Marriage, Peter Kreitler with Bill Bruns. Macmillan Publishing Co., Inc., New York, 1981.

The Social Organization of Sexuality: Sexual Practices in the United States—The complete findings from America's most comprehensive survey of sexual behavior, Edward O. Laumann, John H. Gagnon, Robert T. Michael, and Stuart Michaels. The University of Chicago Press, Chicago, London, 1994.

Adultery: An Analysis of Love and Betrayal, Annette Lawson. Basic Books, Inc., Publishers, New York, 1988.

Secret Lovers; Affairs Happen...How to Cope, Dr. Luann Linquist. Lexington Books, D.C. Heath and Company, Lexington, Toronto, 1989.

The Art of Intimacy, Thomas Patrick Malone. Prentice Hall Press, New York, 1987.

You Only Get Married For the First Time Once, Judy Markey. Doubleday, a division of Bantam Doubleday Dell, New York, 1988 .

The Angry Marriage: Overcoming the Rage, Reclaiming the Love, Bonnie Maslin, Ph.D. Hyperion, New York, 1994.

How to Choose the Wrong Marriage Partner and Live Unhappily Ever After, Robert L. Mason, Jr. and Caroline L. Jacobs. John Knox Press, Atlanta, 1979.

Why Did I Marry You, Anyway? Good Sense & Good Humor in the First Year—and After, Arlene Modica Matthews. Houghton Mifflin, Boston, 1988.

Sex In America A Definitive Survey, Robert T. Michael, John H. Gagnon, Edward O. Laumann, and Gina Kolata. Warner Books, Little Brown and Company, Boston, 1994.

Burning Bridges: Diary of A Mid-Life Affair, Innette Miller. G.P. Putnam's Sons, New York, 1987.

The Total Woman, Marabel Morgan. FH. Revell, New Jersey, 1973.

Extramarital Relations, edited By Gerhard Neubeck. Prentice-Hall Inc., New Jersey, 1969.

How to Succeed In Business and Marriage (For Men Only), Richard W. Ogden. Amacom, New York, 1978.

Caught In the Act the True Adventures of a Divorce Detective; Including the Ten Cardinal Rules for Committing Adultery and Not Getting

Caught, William W. Pearce with William Hoffer. 1976.

The Myth of the Greener Grass A Family Counselor Speaks Frankly About Extramarital Affairs and Offers Both Preventive and Healing Measures, J. Allan Peterson. Tyndale House Publishers, Wheaton, Illinois, 1983.

Monogamy, Adam Phillips. Pantheon Books, a Division of Random House, New York, 1977.

Keeping the Spark Alive Preventing Burnout in Love and Marriage, Ayala M. Pines. St. Martins Press, New York, 1988.

Private Lies Infidelity and the Betrayal of Intimacy, Frank Pittman, M.D. W.W. Norton & Company, New York, London, 1989.

Sexual Arrangements: Marriage and the Temptation of Infidelity, Janet Reibstein, Ph.D. and Martin Richards, Ph.D. Charles Scribner's Sons, Macmillan Publishing Company, New York, 1993.

The Kinsey Institute New Report on Sex: What You Must Know to be Sexually Literate, June M. Reinisch, Ph.D. Director with Ruth Beasley, M.L.S. Edited and Compiled by Debra Kent. St. Martin's Press, New York, 1990 .

The New Other Woman: Contemporary Single Women in Affairs With Married Men, Laurel Richardson. The Free Press, a division of Macmillan, Inc., New York, 1985.

Thinking Divorce? Consider the Shocking Personal and Financial Realities! A Divorce Lawyer Explains Why a Divorce Causes Unexpected Problems and How to Cope With Them. He Also Explains How You May Be Able to Avoid a Divorce., Daniel Z. Shapiro. Almar Press, Binghamton, New York, 1983.

Uncoupling: The Art of Coming Apart A Guide to Sane Divorce, Norman Sheresky and Marya Mannes. Viking Press, New York, 1972.

Growing Through Divorce, Jim Smoke. Harvest House, Irvine, California, 1976.

Triangles: Understanding, Preventing and Surviving an Affair, Lana Staheli, Ph.D. Harper Collins, New York, 1995.

"I Will" The Present and Future of Marriage, Urban G. Steinmetz. Ave Maria Press and Pilgrim Press, Notre Dame and Philadelphia, 1969.

The Extramarital Affair, Herbert S. Strean. The Free Press, a Division of Macmillan Publishing Co., Inc., New York, 1980.

Uncoupling: How Relationships Come Apart, Diane Vaughan. Oxford University Press, Inc., Random House, Inc. New York, 1986.

Independent Women: Work and Community for Single Women 1850-1920, Martha Vicinus. The University of Chicago Press, Chicago, 1985.

How to Get Out of an Unhappy Marriage or an Unhappy Relationship: The Intelligent Woman's and Man's Guide to the Marriage Break by a Noted Clinical Psychologist, Dr. Eugene Walder. Putnam, New York, 1978.

How to Win Back the One You Love: Surefire Strategies from a Best-selling Author and Psychologist, Eric Weber and Steven S. Simring, M.D. Macmillan Publishing Co., Inc., New York, 1983.

Adultery the Forgivable Sin: Healing the Inherited Patterns of Betrayal in Your Family, Bonnie Eaker Weil, Ph.D. with Ruth Winter, Ms. Birch Lane Press, by Carol Publishing Group, New York, 1993.

The American Myth of Success; from Horatio Algar to Norman Vincent Peale, Richard Weiss. Basic Book, New York, 1969.

Playing Around: Women and Extramarital Sex, Linda Wolfe. William Morrow & Company, Inc., New York, 1975.

Psychology: Principles and Applications, Stephen Worchel and Wayne Shebilske. University of Virginia Prentice-Hall, Inc., New Jersey, 1983.

Holy Bible, The New American Bible, containing both the Old and New Testaments, Red Letter Edition, translated from the original languages with the critical use of all the ancient sources by members of the Catholic Biblical Association of America. Thomas Nelson Publishers, Nashville, Camden, New York, 1978

The Oxford Dictionary and Thesaurus, American Edition, Oxford University Press, New York, Oxford, 1996.